Aviation Logistics

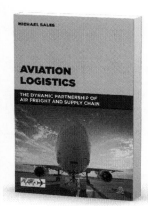

Aviation Logistics
The dynamic partnership of air freight and supply chain

Michael Sales

KoganPage

LONDON PHILADELPHIA NEW DELHI

First published in Great Britain and the United States in 2016 by Kogan Page Limited

2nd Floor, 45 Gee Street	1518 Walnut Street, Suite 1100	4737/23 Ansari Road
London EC1V 3RS	Philadelphia PA 19102	Daryaganj
United Kingdom	USA	New Delhi 110002
www.koganpage.com		India

© Michael Sales, 2016

The right of Michael Sales to be identified as the author of this work has been asserted by him in accordance with the Copyright, Designs and Patents Act 1988.

ISBN   978 0 7494 7270 2
E-ISBN   978 0 7494 7271 9

British Library Cataloguing-in-Publication Data

A CIP record for this book is available from the British Library.

Library of Congress Cataloging-in-Publication Data

CIP data is available.

Library of Congress Control Number: 2015051180

Typeset by Graphicraft Limited, Hong Kong
Print production managed by Jellyfish
Printed and bound by 4edge Limited, UK

CONTENTS

FOREWORD

Having been involved in aviation and especially in the air cargo business, I can say that I have been fortunate to witness the evolution of the cargo transportation and logistics industry. The changes to the current scenario really started from the early 1990s when the science of supply chain management began to develop. Globalization of production and markets placed the focus on finding better production and cost efficiencies. Logistics and transportation became critical to gaining this end and there was a realization that the higher cost of air cargo adds to attaining better cost efficiency within the supply chain. All aspects of the related activities and cost of capital, combined with shorter shelf life of commodities, are affected by the background evolution of the related technology.

I have also had the good fortune to have been around while this change was taking place and being able to contribute and drive some of those changes. On the air transportation side, getting involved in setting up Emirates and Emirates SkyCargo was a real vehicle for driving the changes in how we looked at air cargo transportation and building up services based on the fast-changing requirements of markets and the customers. It was a proud moment to see that the airline became the largest air cargo airline in international operations. I have also been pleased to be involved in founding The International Air Cargo Association, TIACA, which was able to bring together all the elements of the supply chain. These include the transportation/logistics operators, support entities such as the aircraft and other equipment operators, regulators, handlers, various industry associations and organizations and many more entities. Our aim was to create a common voice to help evolve and support commerce as efficiently as possible, as we must never forget that successful commerce depends on the logistics and transportation industry.

Future prospects

The 21st century is a whole new era and a whole new world. It is vital that all aspects of the industry embrace the future and let the future drive today. It is equally critical that all are better aware and equipped to deal with the changes and challenges. The better aware one is, the better equipped one is to not only manage the changes, but also to drive the evolution of our business. Different commodities require different transportation requirements. Gone are the days of one size fits all. Changes in needs are happening in real time these days. The 3D printing is going to bring in a whole plethora of changes to the manufacturing and consumption process. This will trigger changes in many other areas that could create some challenges, but also more new opportunities. We tend to operate in uncharted territory more often than ever. Markets are more volatile and economic cycles tend to linger longer with higher frequency. Those who are able to anticipate change and support the change effectively will be the winners. Developments in the field of the next generation transistor, called the 'memristor' will allow the information technology field to free itself from its traditional dependence on the two-level binary codes to multiple levels, opening up innumerable possibilities, and the evolutionary and the disruptive changes will, combined with the developments in the application of graphene, change the shape and size of electronics and cargo as we know them in the future, giving rise to further miniaturization. Life cycle of items will also become vastly shortened. The highest growth in cargo will be e-commerce-related and those who effectively control the last mile delivery will be the winners of tomorrow.

It is my privilege to introduce this book, *Aviation Logistics*. The authors bring to the fore the various realities of air cargo business and its role in keeping the wheels of commerce rolling. This book is a compilation of looking at various aspects of our business by experts in the field, which guarantees its authority. It is not only very informative and educational but is easy to read and understand. I can recommend it highly for the layperson as well as academia. Aviation and logistics are a great evolving industry to make a career in and as the world becomes smaller and more accessible, they will grow and diversify.

Ram Menen
Former Head of Emirates SkyCargo and
one-time president of TIACA, now retired

WELCOME TO
AVIATION LOGISTICS

I am honoured that several leading and successful figures from the aviation logistics industry have given valuable time and effort to share their knowledge and experience with you and help you to understand this mercurial business sector. There is without doubt much ignorance and many misconceptions about what air cargo contributes to the world economy and much of this, regrettably, is often to be found in the corridors of governments where the desire to heap ever more regulation and taxation upon a struggling industry increases the  sector's difficulty. Aviation has always had many enemies and has suffered badly at the hands of bad weather, earthquakes, tidal waves, wars, fuel price hikes, terrorism, politicians and repressive regulation. Often seen by governments as an easy cash machine and a target for scoring cheap environmental points, air cargo feeds the world with produce, medicines, clothing and industrial equipment.

Transport accounts for a high proportion of the final cost of the product, in some cases up to 40 per cent. Due to the varied factors involved, international consignments clearly demand a careful and detailed costing. The choice of transport mode will depend on the type of goods, the urgency of delivery and the destination. Frequently there will be a combination of some or all of these to form eventually a major component of the total supply chain. Intermediate warehousing, repackaging and partial assembly may also be part of the process. The decision to employ air cargo is based on a number of factors, including urgency, value of shipment, protective environment, access and product shelf life. Price is not the only consideration as some products are needed urgently as in the case of a broken machine needing a new part or a consignment of fresh seafood as well as the market demand of a new fashion.

Many people are not aware that much of what we need to sustain our lifestyle, including energy, communications, pharmaceuticals, food, flowers, entertainment, clothes and transport depend substantially on the air cargo logistics supply chain that works alongside all other transport modes. In this book, we have provided the practical knowledge and explanations about the processes involved and the vital role played by the air cargo industry in maintaining the global logistics supply chain. The choice of air cargo is not only reserved for high-value commodities or perishable items, but includes just about everything that touches our lives. If you like F1 motor racing, symphony concerts, strawberries at Christmas, the latest fashions or you need diabetic drugs and medication, air freight will be acting on your behalf behind the scenes. At the same time, protecting the environment is one of the industry's top priorities. Aviation and air transport account for 3 per cent of global carbon emissions, which we review in detail in the chapter on environment. Aviation is a source for goods that connects people around the world; for example, it delivers agricultural produce from Africa and the Far East to South America. It facilitates trade and is the only industry that has globally committed to specific actions to neutralize carbon emission growth by 2020 and reduce emissions by 50 per cent by 2050. The fast-evolving global economy is connected by events that impact on us within hours, not days. We have seen over the last few years the economic growth of countries such as Brazil, Russia, India, China and South Africa (BRICS). As these countries and other developing nations begin to compete and attract foreign direct investment, we witness their increasing prosperity and new emerging middle classes. That is manifesting itself in the demand for branded consumer goods, travel and leisure activities.

Security has become a major part of air cargo and has evolved further since the terrorist attack on New York's Twin Towers on 9/11. There have been countless other criminal assaults on cargo shipments of cash and valuables over the years and today, considering the high value of goods moving by air, such as computers, mobile phones, fashion, pharmaceuticals and diamonds, nearly every shipment can be considered as a potential target. The temptation and opportunities are greater than ever and the problem is exacerbated in many cases by reluctance on the part of the victims to report the crime or even acknowledge its occurrence.

Cargo theft affects everyone as it damages economies and companies, forces up prices and feeds the world's black markets that are often sources of funding for terrorists and large criminal gangs. In the United States alone, it is estimated that some $30 billion worth of cargo is stolen annually by highly sophisticated and well-organized gangs. Cargo is at its most vulnerable when it is on the ground, especially in transit by road. Trucking companies may respond by raising prices or employing expensive security guards, the costs of which will be passed on to customers.

The main challenge facing this industry now is the implementation of electronic cargo processing (e-freight), which would speed up the entire air freight chain as well as increasing security and cutting a great deal of cost. It has been taking and will continue to take a long time to gain acceptance by the whole industry but as of summer 2014 an estimated 14 per cent of international shipments were processed electronically, led by Emirates, Cathay Pacific and Korean Air airlines, as well as leading logistics companies. I sincerely hope you enjoy this book and I urge you to visit the various websites we have listed where you will find more details, facts and figures.

As I write this, the world is embroiled in conflicts in Iraq, Syria, Libya and Ukraine. The possibility of trade barriers between Russia and Europe could result in a return to Cold War routes that are longer and more expensive to operate than the trans-Russia route. Aviation is never without challenge and threat, but it goes on and continues to deliver people and cargo throughout the world.

Acknowledgements

Thanks so much to my colleagues who have contributed to this book. A special thanks goes to Stan Wraight, whose technical knowledge has been indispensable.

Air cargo – trying harder

Aviation is a vital component of the global economy, involving some 60 million jobs and generating over US$2.2 trillion of economic activity. The need to travel, whether for business or leisure, has expanded the capacity and scale of aircraft size.

Aircraft manufacturers are working continuously to create bigger, better, quieter and more fuel-efficient products to satisfy this growing appetite. The development of the air cargo industry has simultaneously driven the global market for goods including electronics, pharmaceuticals, flowers, fruit and industrial components. We are constantly reminded that around 35 per cent of the world's total cargo traffic value is classified as air cargo.

The industry embraces a wide range of products and shipment sizes to cater for all customer needs, employing different appropriate aircraft. At one end of the spectrum on regional or domestic markets, international post, newspapers and documents, food and essential medical supplies are often transported in very small aircraft such Metro SW4 (for example to service the many Greek islands every day). A major proportion of air freighted goods travel in the bellies of passenger planes, such as Boeing 777 or Airbus 330/340, which have the capacity for 25 tons when fully loaded with passengers and baggage. Medium-sized freighter aircraft such as B737, A300-600, B767 and large freighter aircraft such B747-400 and B747-8 transport every kind of product, including fresh flowers, mobile phones, medicines and live animals.

At the other end of the scale is the giant Antonov. Based originally on a military transport plane, it is capable of carrying up to a 150 metric tonne payload. Since the era of the Zeppelin, experiments continue to develop airships that theoretically could carry much bigger loads at lower cost. Whether these can be harnessed for efficient cargo transport is yet to be seen.

The benefits of the global connectivity achieved by both ocean and air transport reach practically every type of modern industry and business and

FIGURE 1.1 AN-124 loading outsize cargo

are an essential ingredient of the global supply chain. According to Tony Tyler, CEO of IATA, by 2030 the number of airline passengers will probably double and cargo traffic could reach 150 million tons per year, supporting some 80 million jobs and US$6.9 million of global GDP.

Thanks to the mix of pressures in aviation including spikes in fuel prices, fierce competition from other transport modes, economic fluctuations, war, weather and environmental issues, air cargo operators and ground service providers are forever striving to offer a better service at a lower price. This balance becomes almost impossible if quality is to be maintained. The integrators have for many years led the way by providing rapid door-to-door overnight service but at an extremely high price.

At first the express market was mostly limited to mail, important documents and small packages but today the original business models have evolved into total freight and express/postal operators, even including trucking networks and ocean shipping. Because these operators have controlled the whole process within their own in-house computer, handling and transport systems, they have complete control and can track the progress of any individual shipment.

The traditional air cargo players, however, are obliged to work through many different partners and are often reluctant, because of low margins, to invest in modern methods. The need to follow the example of companies such as Federal Express and DHL and their use of computer-based processing, which is the number-one priority of IATA and TIACA, or projects such as e-freight, will never materialize without firm commitment from the industry, and the transport time associated with scheduled carriers will remain uncompetitive.

There is no doubt that airlines increasingly view cargo today as a vital contributor to their profitability and total service package, yet very few look at it as a core business. With the introduction of a new generation of wide-bodied passenger aircraft, a significant amount of cargo can be loaded on nearly every flight, even with a full passenger load. Skilled handling and loading can increase the amounts flown in bellies. However, given the constraints of regulations and cost, it is increasingly difficult to maintain ground and warehouse handling as a profitable activity in-house, so out-sourcing is the standard model for airlines these days.

Unfortunately, most airlines view ground handling as a comparatively low-level function, which must be inexpensive but still maintain high qual-ity – a contradiction in terms and one that exacerbates the problems. Many of the industry awards for 'best airline' are the result of excellent ground handling, the only place where product differentiation can take place.

To achieve a fast, quality operation there must be a substantial invest-ment in equipment, buildings, technology, staff and training, and this requires capital investment, which ground handling companies have difficulty justifying if the airlines are not willing to pay a fair return. With airlines constantly demanding keener prices, more facilities and better quality, this equation becomes almost unworkable. Basic costs of ground and shed handling are increasing remorselessly by 2–3 per cent per year on average.

At the 2014 world Cargo Symposium in Los Angeles, Des Vertannes, Global Head of Cargo at IATA, stressed the need for the air freight in-dustry to cut 48 hours off the current process time and thus become more efficient and attractive to shippers. It is astonishing that despite new aircraft, technology and sophisticated integrated logistics, the average time taken to move goods by air – six to seven days – has remained the same for some 40 years! This 48 hour reduction target by 2020 has to work alongside the target of making everyone operate with electronic processing; to date this has been adopted by only 12 per cent of the market. And it can only work if a partnership between the airline and ground handling companies can be forged. He urged the industry to provide the premium service for which the customers are paying. It was suggested that the wider use of frequent belly hold cargo capacity could go a long way towards achieving these goals.

The use of freighter aircraft has changed considerably since the 2008 recession, when demands for manufactured products fell dramatically on a global scale, and passenger aircraft with enormous cargo capacity were being delivered to airlines around the world. You can read about the movement away from freighter aircraft in Chapter 3; briefly the weaknesses of the freighter business model are easy to identify but complex to solve.

One use of freighters has been the charter market, which meets specific customer needs. When a freighter is chartered to transport goods to one particular destination at a very keen price but with no return cargo, the aircraft must return empty, which is obviously a loss, forcing the operator to seek a return cargo at any price. If, however, the operator runs a scheduled route structure, there will be as much freight returning as the outbound through dedicated business planning. A good example of this process in action is the Luxembourg-based all-cargo airlines Cargolux, which has for many years operated regular scheduled services to many destinations throughout the world.

The passenger aircraft by contrast is flying on a regular scheduled route with or without cargo on board and thus does not have the return load business problem to the same extent. However, hard selling by the airline's cargo sales force is required to fill the bellies in a highly competitive market; this is often done on the basis of contribution pricing only, not taking into account the true costs of flying that a freighter operator must bear.

Volatile and sky-high fuel prices, coupled with some extreme natural events, wars and acts of terrorism, have devastated the margins of cargo operators over the last 20 years. Despite all the debated shortcomings of the industry, however, the entrepreneurial culture of its leaders has found solutions to most of these challenges and air cargo is still the first choice for shippers seeking fast and safe transport of their precious goods.

Another advantage passenger airlines have is that, due to the scale of their operations, they can continue to buy or lease the latest and most up to date aircraft costing several hundred million dollars but with much better fuel and emissions performance. Emirates Airlines, for example, has a fleet of 265 new or about to be renewed aircraft including a large fleet of B777-300, Airbus A380-800s and plans a total fleet of 400 mixed wide bodies by 2020. The airline also has a fleet of 14 wide-bodied freighters. Very few all-cargo operators can even think of this level of investment. With a Boeing 777 being capable of carrying 25 tons of cargo in addition to a full load of passengers plus baggage, it is clear that shippers will be attracted to this option. A carrier like Emirates is able to offer network scale and flexibility that no freighter carrier, even Cargolux, can dream of matching. Cargo aircraft are often unwelcome at large overcrowded airport hubs, especially at night, and restrictions are in place at airports such as Heathrow, Frankfurt and Beijing. This has engendered a number of 'cargo friendly' airports that are eager to accept this traffic.

FIGURE 1.2   B777 highly efficient cargo carrier

Supply chains under pressure

In one decade the internet revolution has changed the face of manufacturing and distribution beyond recognition. The logistics business and especially air cargo is having to renew itself to accommodate new rules, technologies and market demands. Heavier security also has the effect of slowing down processes and there is also the failure of many players in the business to take innovation on board or make the necessary investment in facilities, staff and training.

E-commerce with its 'I want it now' culture puts intense pressure on efficiency, distribution and final delivery. Technology speeds up the process with faster Customs clearance, lighter documentation and tracking, but this is mostly handled by the postal authorities, not airlines. In the future, technology will bring more transparency and make information available when needed; at that point the airlines could get back in the game. E-commerce will facilitate better profiling and help speed up security and Customs clearance. Attaching X-ray images will help with screening and will cut back on the need for manual intervention. If all goes to plan the entire supply chain process should be 100 per cent electronic within five to 10 years. The arrival of seamless multimodal transactions should become a reality.

There is, however, a danger that too much theory and computer-based decisions could adversely affect the physical flow of day-to-day work, and the skill sets needed in the staff and management of both airlines and ground handling companies. Future managers must have training and hands-on experience of document processing, building pallets, loading an aircraft or checking dangerous goods processing, or they will not be able to maximize the progress of cargo as leaders. Some dirty hands are necessary.

Thanks to the rapid development of products, especially high-tech items (telecom, TV, etc), product life is being dramatically reduced. As far as the supply chain is concerned, nobody is willing to hold stock, which changes the whole inventory management dynamic. The industry-wide acceptance of electronic communications, especially the e-air waybill, will lay the foundations for the eventual paperless air cargo process. For those shippers that choose air transport, speed is critical but has to be paid for.

The air cargo industry must therefore continue to minimize costs and cut processing time while always being innovative and responsive, creative and a leader, or there will be a continuing shift to ocean transport as industries such as automotive find this more suited to their needs. It is estimated that over 400,000 tons have been lost to ocean each year since 2000. We must as an industry get ourselves back on track, and treat air cargo as a core business.

Despite all this, air cargo has been growing by an average of 2.6 per cent in the past year. Our objective must be to achieve much higher growth levels to tackle the overcapacity issues brought on by new passenger aircraft deliveries, and beyond that to achieve profitability that would fund investments.

Air cargo's strengths

Air transport brings several unique selling points to the supply chain:

- Just-in-time (JIT) has cut the amount of inventory and expensive warehousing of previous eras due to rapid air transport.
- The high value of some shipments and their vulnerability to theft, counterfeiting and temperature make it vital to deliver quickly by air, at the same time allowing the shipper to realize the financial benefit more quickly.
- The rapid delivery of spare parts to maintain an industrial process. This may involve a simple component or major oil drilling replacement tool. Downtime in such instances can create huge losses.
- Perishables and pharmaceuticals need fast and temperature-controlled environments and at the same time must meet the requirements of health regulations.

As society changes ever faster, air cargo will continue to be a growth industry catering for the needs not only of traditional Western consumers but also a new generation of wealthy Chinese, Asian and South American middle classes, whose spending power is very significant. Closer across-the-board collaboration between suppliers, shippers and transporters will be essential to deliver a level of service to satisfy customers.

Modal shift

The subject of modal shift is on the logistics industry's collective mind and has received much coverage in the trade press. It is being blamed for the underperformance of air cargo and is being attributed with some 30 per cent of the loss in air share. As we move towards greater standardization of commodity shipping, air cargo operators are having to face up to this trend. In terms of weight, air trade represents 1.7 per cent of containerized traffic but in value it is estimated to represent around 35 per cent. However, many of the traditional air products are now being partially switched to ocean freight. The increase in ocean may be attributed in part to new ways of manufacturing and distribution plus the natural growth of demand for goods that will always travel by sea. Despite the losses by air cargo to ocean, high-tech, fashion, capital equipment, machinery parts and automotive are maintaining growth, albeit slow.

The introduction of controlled atmosphere containers (CAC) is allowing some perishables to be moved by ocean. Fruit and vegetables, from the moment of harvest, start to consume oxygen and produce carbon dioxide and ethylene gas. In any form of container they will release moisture and generate heat. These factors cause the produce to deteriorate, which in turn cuts the shelf life at the consumer end. The faster transport provided by air compensates for this. However, with the use of CAC, which include devices for delaying these processes, a much bigger proportion of perishable produce can travel by sea (see Chapter 8 on the cool chain). This has resulted in air cargo losing market share to its ocean competitor and is a major concern of the airlines but not necessarily the forwarders, which use all modes of transport.

Freighter aircraft are indispensable for some air freight logistics traffic: for example shipments of zoo animals, music groups, museum exhibits, F1 cars, racehorses and many more (see Chapter 10 on special cargoes). The success of aviation logistics in the future will depend on the flexibility and enterprise of its managers and their willingness to embrace new technologies and ideas.

The world of air cargo

02

OLIVER EVANS, former Chairman
The International Air Cargo Association (TIACA)

Oliver Evans

You are young and ambitious. You are born into a generation that has seen a phenomenal expansion of new technological solutions in industries as various as medicine, consumer electronics and transportation, to name but a few. Globalization has seen manufacture and assembly spread all over the world so that global trade has expanded hugely. Millions have benefited from this trade and living standards have reached unprecedented heights not only in the developed world but also in rapidly rising new economies. And millions have migrated in search of jobs and opportunities, from the countryside to the city and from country to country, or continent to continent. No other industry facilitates and drives that global trade more than air cargo. No other industry offers you better opportunities to be engaged with these exciting developments, in daily contact with people from all over the world, solving global supply chain problems, using your creativity for the widest range of tasks.

It is therefore ironic that the air cargo industry has struggled to make itself known to a wider public, let alone understood and appreciated. The phenomenal volumes of air trade have long dictated that airlines invest in all-cargo airplanes to supplement the space available in the belly of passenger aircraft, but the industry has remained in the shadow of the larger passenger business. At most airlines, CEOs have remained focused on the passenger business and have considered cargo merely a by-product, thereby simultaneously undervaluing the product and underinvesting in it. Happily the challenges to profitability in the airline industry as a whole mean that this naïve and harmful neglect is changing. Increasingly, cargo is being recognized as critical to profitability, and the most enlightened airlines are investing heavily in their cargo business, whether in recruitment, processes or infrastructure. Let us focus then on each of the three key dimensions of our industry that ensure its long-term future and sustainability:

1 Profit, or the ability to attract funds and invest them in an appropriate way.

2 Planet, or the social and ecological impact our activities have on the environment.

3 People, who use our tools, design our processes, analyse the past, manage the present and shape the future.

Profit

Tackling profit first: our industry is asset-rich and requires massive investment in aircraft and infrastructure. The airline industry transports goods that amount to barely 1 per cent of the volume of international trade, but well over 35 per cent of the value of trade, a proportion that is rising constantly as manufactured products increase in sophistication. Moreover these goods, whether they are end products for consumption or components for assembly, are traded by the widest range of industries and come in every shape and size, in fact any that will fit the contours of an airplane. The goods also require different conditions of transport, from high security for valuables, to a temperature-controlled environment for perishables and pharmaceuticals, or express transit times for all urgent shipments. A multitude of documents, from air waybills to all kinds of declarations (of security, payment, origin, etc) accompany the shipments. Consolidation, storage and deconsolidation take place at different stages of the transportation according to customer and carrier requirements. Finally many different parties are involved, from forwarders to airlines, IT companies and handlers, truckers and regulators. The supply chain is highly complex, sophisticated, expensive and critical.

Investments are massive, and profitability correspondingly elusive. This is partly because the industry is so fragmented, but also because aircraft and capacity tend to be ordered when times are good, and simultaneously by all key players, and delivered when the market has moved on, rather than at optimal times from the point of view of demand. The industry, in short, is highly cyclical and fragile. This situation calls for innovation, or indeed disruption. As the flow of information in the supply chain is as critical as the flow of goods, it is perhaps surprising that no IT company has positioned itself as a 'virtual integrator' making shipment data (owner, consignee, nature and quantity of goods, etc) available to any party requiring the information at the right time and the right place. This availability of information, to the industry and to regulators, is surely the future. It will streamline processes massively, improve quality and reliability, replace paper documents with electronic ones or eliminate their necessity altogether. Billions will be saved by the industry, and by its users. Perhaps the disruption hasn't happened yet precisely because of the complexity and fragmentation of the industry, which have functioned as a barrier to new entrants: the IT companies serving our industry are born in our industry and many are spin-offs from airlines' IT divisions. For this and other reasons, progress towards e-freight has been painfully slow and industry targets have been reset time and time again.

Average end-to-end transport time for goods by air has also remained stubbornly around six and a half days, even though it takes less than 24 hours in flying time to connect any two points on our planet. Integrators meanwhile have much shorter dwell times on the ground, and achieve greater reliability, than the best standards of air cargo. Despite this, the expense, rigidity and limitations of their systems mean that they only fulfil some of shippers' needs, so that the airline–forwarder combination continues to enjoy a large share of the total air cake. This is why it is so important for the air cargo industry to act in concert to overcome regulatory or other common barriers, while innovating and competing fiercely with their own business models. Happily there is every sign that the most enlightened leaders and companies are doing just that, and we are entering an era of exciting transformation.

Planet

Turning now to the second pillar of sustainability, planet, it has to be acknowledged that, shamefully, the issue has often been considered as only of peripheral relevance, or worse still as a marketing gimmick. Despite increasingly strident IPCC (International Panel on Climate Change) reports demonstrating the overwhelming evidence of the impact of human activity on the environment, the information quickly disappears from newspaper or television headlines. ICAO (The International Civil Aviation Organization) has finally agreed a framework for the establishment of a global emissions trading scheme (ETS), but it is far from acceptance or implementation by individual member states.

Because of the slow progress, the EU attempted to unilaterally introduce an ETS of its own, which led to an outcry by the aviation industry, and by other states, because it would have created market distortions, and gone way beyond the EU's area of jurisdiction. The EU, also thanks to the efforts of industry associations like TIACA, later withdrew the plan, but the issue is far from resolved.

Meanwhile the air cargo industry is fond of repeating that it is responsible for 'only around 2 per cent' of global CO_2 emissions, as if this were not a huge quantity in its own right (688 million tonnes in 2013). The simple, undeniable, fact is that aviation's emissions are considerably higher per ton kilometre than other modes of transport. Therefore a great responsibility rests upon the shoulders of the leadership of our industry. However, it should be noted that around 80 per cent of aviation CO_2 is emitted from flights over 1,500 kilometres in length, for which there is no practical alternative form of transport in a globalized world of just-in-time supply chains. Instead, the industry has set itself very ambitious climate targets, to improve its fleet fuel efficiency by an average of 1.5 per cent per annum between 2009 and 2020; to stabilize net carbon emissions from 2020 by capping them through carbon-neutral growth; and by 2050, net emissions will be half what they were in 2005. This sounds, and is, very ambitious, but it should be remembered that the industry has already reduced emissions per ton kilometre by more than 70 per cent, and perceived noise by more than 75 per cent, since the first jet aircraft. This is made possible by massive investment in new aircraft and technology.

Modern engines consume a fraction of the fuel they used to. Successful experiments have been carried out with biofuels and other sustainable fuels, and industrial exploitation will follow when it becomes economically viable. Recycling, of parts or entire old aircraft, has become normal.

These important investments by the airlines themselves are only part of the picture of sustainability in the air cargo industry. Flight paths are made more efficient. Capacity utilization is improved. Ground processes are streamlined and infrastructure better utilized. The technological progress involved is rapid and dazzling.

Above all, the air cargo industry, in a globalized world, offers the possibilities for companies in all other industries to transform their own business models, and thereby their supply chains, to meet their own sustainability goals. Certain, lower-valued commodities have shifted to surface transport, but high-value components are delivered just-in-time. Products reach new markets and create new benefits. No other industry powers global economic growth and transformation to the same extent, creating employment, trade links and support for sustainable development throughout the world.

Certain countries, mostly but not exclusively in the Middle East, have made aviation and air cargo part of a government strategy to boost awareness, recognition and even admiration for their respective countries. Taken in aggregate, an expanding and advancing air cargo industry yields benefits that are shared globally. In short, concern for the planet is about far more than a 'green agenda' or promotion. It is about invention, indeed constant innovation and reinvention. Constant improvement. And an awareness of the bigger picture, of the effects and side effects of any industrial process or application of technology.

People

It is now time to consider the role of people in driving the air cargo business, and at the heart of the sustainability model. Cargo has long been considered a very 'operational' area of business, especially when compared to the more glamorous world of passengers and travel. To the outsider, cargo (if considered at all) seemed driven by experts, and characterized by complex, rigid processes. We ourselves have perpetuated this image by focusing our various training and induction programmes on the technical aspects of the business: how to draw up a house waybill, or an air waybill; how to calculate transport charges; how to build a consolidation; how to ensure security and safety norms, whether governmental or company-specific. There were and are many such courses, offered by companies themselves or by industry associations. Their assumption is that cargo is a 'trade' to be learnt, and then perpetually executed. Of course the kind of knowledge imparted during such courses has a role to play in the industry. Of course compliance and safety are essential and not to be compromised. Of course processes must be understood in order to be executed correctly. The IT systems that supported them were correspondingly rigid and not transparent. You simply had to learn by rote all the steps that constituted a booking, or a status update. But for all the reasons outlined in preceding paragraphs, the industry and environment are changing very rapidly.

It is people who look beyond the borders of the industry to understand the changing needs and demands of customers. It is people who create a vision of where the industry is heading. It is people who organize themselves in teams and partnerships to plan and implement changes. Aircraft can be bought by anybody: infrastructure can be built by anybody. Processes, and the products that are delivered by them, can be copied by anybody.

But in a world of high complexity like ours, in a world where many different documents accompany each shipment, in a world where many different companies collaborate to deliver a single shipment, in a world in which urgency is king, and last-minute arrangements the norm, things do go wrong on an all-too-frequent basis. This is when companies truly differentiate themselves by the attitude and motivation of their staff. This is when it is clear that air cargo is a people business, and success is based on trust and collaboration.

The most important responsibility for the leadership of the air cargo industry is to attract, retain and motivate the best staff and managers. The industry needs people who are endlessly curious; willing to learn about the limitless range of other industries that rely upon us for their supply chain; willing to change even successful past practices, if the need arises to innovate; willing to take risks, and to take responsibility for the outcome of their decisions and actions. A constant of any job in our industry is collaboration and teamwork: creating trust through respect and good listening skills. Traditionally education courses were geared towards one particular job specialization, whether sales or operational. They were delivered by the company or by institutions, but always with a narrow focus. Fortunately this is changing, and associations like TIACA are developing leadership courses aiming to bring together practitioners not only of various roles within a company, but also from different companies or entities functioning across the supply chain: regulators, banks, Customs, freight forwarders, airlines, ground handlers, truckers, IT companies. A proper understanding of each other's view, role and competences is essential.

All these different elements constitute sustainability for the air cargo industry. The transport of goods and mail was the first goal of the airline industry: the pioneers flew their primitive aircraft in search of glory, certainly, but also to deliver mail and parcels all over the world. They wanted to connect people and industries, and to make money by doing so. Soon the passenger industry was born, and people wanted to fly to see the world, or to conduct their business. But cargo (and mail) has remained an essential, if unsung, aspect of the aviation industry.

The range of commodities transported is truly astounding: live animals (pets, farm or zoo animals), live human organs, advanced pharmaceuticals or medical equipment, valuables (banknotes, precious metals, luxury goods), products of every size and type imaginable, traded by every industry that exists around the world. Not only are the value and sensitivity of certain goods so high as to necessitate the shortest transit time, but situations regularly arise in which low-value commodities require shipment by air, whether due to emergency (as in a natural or man-made disaster), a surge in demand or production irregularity. Despite the fact that certain products like computers, which used to be carried by air, now typically are transported by sea, human invention and the constant – and accelerating – pipeline of new, increasingly sophisticated and delicate products mean that the future of the air cargo industry is bright – at least for those companies that are alert to changes and new developments.

A wind of change is blowing through the industry. Regulators, who used to design and implement new regulations with little regard to the users and consequences, are now consulting us and involving us in pilot projects and common studies. They have recognized that the best of rules is useless unless it is practicable and understood by those who have to implement it. They have come to understand that their own goals (compliance with government directives towards safe and open trade) correspond precisely to those of industry. They know that air cargo is an essential engine of global trade and consumption.

The industry itself has gained in confidence. We have started to look beyond the confines of our own world. We have become more articulate about the benefits of our activities to society as a whole. We have developed new and more open leadership programmes. We have started to attract a new generation of future leaders, young people eager to make a difference in a globalized world. In a global industry, we have started to embrace diversity, whether of gender, culture, or experience.

The challenges we face have never been greater. The world is ever more interconnected and interdependent. Our safety and security record is remarkable considering the proliferation of terrorist groups of one shade or another. Our procedures have been revised, tested and strengthened after each incident or near-incident, so that very few lives, airplanes or goods have been lost considering the millions of flights that take place every year. We have invested in screening, whether it is physical or the multiple layers of intelligence that play such a vital role in thwarting potential enemies. But just as we seem to have become adept at always staying one step ahead of them, thus ensuring the safety of crew, passengers and goods, we are becoming ever more vulnerable to a new type of threat: cyber attacks. We are pumping out and sharing ever increasing amounts of data. Yet we have not thought through the good types of usage to which all this data can be put, or the bad.

The human impact on the planet is there for all to see, in the smog that lies above certain rapidly growing cities, or the rubbish-strewn streets of suburbs the world over. Waste plastic is accumulating in floating plates in the middle of the Pacific Ocean which are as big as an average European country. Shortages of many natural products, food or even water are emerging. Above all, the climate is changing in unpredictable ways, and dire consequences are only starting to be investigated.

There is no way back to a society of hunter gatherers, living in harmony with their environment, self-sufficient and innocent, totally ignorant of the world beyond the borders of their village or community. We are endowed with intelligence and insatiable curiosity, and we have always been driven to explore, to investigate, to develop. Groups started to meet each other, specialize and trade. In time came new forms of transport, including ours, air transport. This will continue into the future, and new forms of transport will come to challenge the aircraft we know today: airships, or unmanned vehicles. Most likely they will only provide more choice, and they will complement the possibilities of today, not replace them.

People speak of the future as if there were just one out there, waiting to happen. In fact we should speak of futures, because our decisions and actions determine which of many possible futures finally comes about. We are the agents of change and of development. We are responsible for our environment and for our planet. We are responsible for the welfare of our descendants and of all the creatures that share this world with us. Air cargo, as the engine of modern trade and development, has a vital role to play in determining how we will cope with all of the challenges of today and of tomorrow. You will not join a more exciting industry.

TIACA

The air cargo industry is responsible for the safe and reliable transport of $6.5 trillion of goods annually, goods that are traded by every industry imaginable and that come in all shapes and sizes. This requires the fulfilment of a wide range of conditions of transport, from constant, specific temperature ranges to enhanced speed or security. The industry is truly global and highly fragmented, complex and challenged by economic, technological, environmental and regulatory factors. TIACA is the only global association open to all stakeholders in the industry and counts shippers, forwarders, airlines, integrators, handlers, IT providers, truckers and educational institutes amongst its membership. TIACA is a not-for-profit organization that reinvests 100 per cent of its income in promoting and supporting its members and the vital role they play in world commerce. Our activities fall under three major headings: advocacy and industry affairs, networking and the organization of events, and education and knowledge sharing. TIACA therefore fulfils a unique and vital role as the voice of the industry, engaging with regulators and responding to the demands of shippers. While various segments of the industry are well represented by their own associations, we require a collaborative approach in order to facilitate a sustainable and connected global industry. TIACA is the global organization for all users and participants in the air cargo industry.

Air cargo history

03

It is generally agreed that commercial aviation began its life around 1910/11 when the US Post Office Department recognized the possibility of developing aircraft into a practicable means of mail transportation. It took many years for this to become a real transportation solution, as aircraft were very primitive, with little capacity or range. However, the First World War generated more efficient aircraft and after the War many people attempted to start airline operations using ex-military equipment. Although very cheap to acquire, these machines incurred very high operating and maintenance costs, unaffordable for commercial operations. These planes, therefore, demanded modification and newer engines and designs. The other severe limitation was that in order to operate regular and reliable services, some basic but essential supporting ground and navigation services were needed. These included airports with proper runways, repair shops, connecting roads, handling facilities, as well as weather and flight controls. In most cases, these did not materialize for many years. Most important of all, sufficient paid traffic was needed to achieve commercial viability. Mail delivery, domestic and international, accounted for over half of the nascent industry's income from 1918 to 1939. In addition, commercial aviation was not a profitable activity on its own and needed financial support from subsidies and high postal fees. Finally, it was impossible to operate legally across international boundaries without acceptable rules.

Regulations and agreements

To meet this requirement, several conventions and agreements were introduced to cover the new aviation sector. The Paris International Air Convention, introduced in 1922, defined the sovereign control of national airspace. The principle of freedom to fly over a country's airspace was generally accepted. This treaty, containing nine separate chapters, also dealt with nationality of aircraft, certificates of airworthiness, patents and permissions for take-off and landing. The International Commission of Air Navigation (ICAN), based in Paris, introduced a raft of legal, technical and meteorological services when representatives of 43 countries attended a conference in Paris in October 1925. Gradually, air travel was being accepted as a reliable means of transport.

During 1926, the newly formed German Lufthansa company transported some 1,000 tons of air cargo as well as 6,000 passengers. The new route network was soon followed by cooperation with the German national railway system and in 1927 the over-the-counter market came into existence. While Lufthansa aircraft transported air cargo on its route network, the German railway took over the ground feeder services.

Another aviation milestone was the Warsaw Convention, which was signed in 1929 by 152 different parties and came into force in 1933; it was the most important agreement of the aviation industry at that time. It set out to regulate liability for international carriage of people, luggage or goods performed by aircraft for reward. It defined international carriage, the rules concerning documentation, the liability limitations of the carrier as well as rules governing jurisdiction. In 1955, following a review by ICAO, The Hague Protocol was adopted by the ICAO council. In 1955, the two conventions were merged into the Warsaw Convention, as amended in 1955, and then in 1999 the Montreal Convention replaced it. The Montreal Convention (formally, the Convention for the Unification of Certain Rules for International Carriage by Air) is a multilateral treaty adopted by a diplomatic meeting of ICAO member states in 1999. It amended important provisions of the Warsaw Convention's regime. The Convention sought to bring uniform and predictable rules on the international carriage of passengers, baggage and cargo.

World War II witnessed major improvements in aviation technology. The aircraft were vital for military purposes as well as heavy cargo transport. Most of these aircraft had little practical civil application, but the capabilities of the manufacturers were tested and developed during this era. Having put their machines to the ultimate test, the resulting generation of aircraft was ready for a new reliable role in civil air transport.

At first, cargo on long-haul international routes remained at a modest level and consisted mostly of priority airmail, which did not require large capacity. KLM, Deutsche Lufthansa and Air France were the pioneers, carrying newspapers, banknotes and gold bullion, perfume and fashion items, spare parts for machinery and live animals, including racing pigeons. KLM was first in the transport of large animals, such as horses and cows, as well as fresh flowers. Most freighter aircraft used at this time were either converted passenger aircraft with the seats removed, or ex-military aircraft that had long proved to be suitable for the task. Air travel started to expand

and cargo capacity was needed to supply post-war rebuilding efforts. New types of aircraft were developed, starting with turboprop engines; shortly afterwards came the introduction of commercial jet aircraft. Again, it was the development of military aircraft that led the way for the civil sector to develop.

The Berlin airlift

A significant milestone in air freight progress was what became known as the Berlin airlift. After World War II, the former Allied forces – France, the United Kingdom, the USSR and the United States, shared the control of Germany. Berlin, which was within the overall Soviet territory, was also split as a city between the four powers. In the summer of 1948, USSR leader Joseph Stalin, feeling threatened by the US presence in Berlin, decided to take control of the city and blockaded the Western section, cutting off access to food and supplies. In what would become the first major confrontation of the Cold War, US President Harry Truman made the historic decision to supply Berlin by air. In a heroic joint effort, the Americans and British delivered more than 2 million tons of supplies to the beleaguered city over the next 10 months, eventually forcing Stalin to give up his blockade.

The city of Berlin became the focal point of the post-war political standoff between the Western allies and the Russians. In order to supply the 2 million citizens of Berlin with almost everything necessary for their daily life, US

FIGURE 3.1   Flying in supplies to besieged Berlin

and British pilots flew day and night to land urgently required supplies of food, coal, medicines and other essential necessities.

The runways available in West Berlin, especially at the Templehof airfield in the US sector, were not sufficient to land large cargo aircraft safely, so plans were made to build a new airfield in the French sector. All of the equipment and materials for the new runways had to be flown in. The United States provided a fleet of around 35 C-54 aircraft, the military version of the DC-4, with two squadrons of Sunderland flying boats based at Lake Havel in Berlin. When in full swing, around 260 US and British aircraft were ferrying the targeted 4,500 tons of supplies daily. This eventually rose to some 8,000 tons a day. The aircraft flew so frequently and were so densely scheduled that they often became stacked above the city in a dangerous holding pattern. The airlift moved a total of 2,325,000 tons of essential supplies during the 15-month period it was in operation. It is estimated that 621 aircraft took part in the airlift, operating 270,000 flights with a total distance of over 124.5 million miles flown. The blockade of Berlin highlighted the conflicting pressures of keeping costs down while fulfilling customers' needs, still present in the ever-changing challenge of successful air cargo operations in today's fluctuating world economy.

The growth of air freight

It is generally agreed that the Berlin airlift was the first occasion when air freight was employed to maximum effect. Aircraft, ground handlers and crews were forced to breaking point and many lessons were learnt that were carried through into the next decades of commercial air freight operations.

The coming decades saw the growth in air cargo as a viable commercial tool becoming a reality. A number of aircraft types were in use during the 1950s and 1960s, but what was needed was a custom-built aircraft suitable for the task. The aircraft would require a strong floor with roller beds for sliding heavy pallets, a lifting front nose cone or retractable back ramp, and a high interior cabin ceiling. All of this was needed to allow fast and efficient loading and unloading: aircraft do not make money on the ground.

Very few airports were willing to invest in the necessary ground-handling facilities that cargo desperately needed. As the added value of freight traffic became recognized, investment in cargo facilities spread around the world, led by airports such as Hong Kong, Singapore, Miami, New York and Dubai. Vast improvements in Customs procedures and electronic documentation have, over the last 20 years, pushed the industry into quicker and more competitive ways.

The jet age

The air freight industry, as we know it today, was revolutionized by the arrival of a new generation of jet aircraft, the DC-8 and Boeing 707, capable of cruising speeds of around 550 mph with a payload in the freighter version of up to 40 metric tonnes. The invention of special freight containers called unit load device (ULD) heralded faster and more controllable loading/ unloading and a more efficient use of available space (see Figure 3.2). These containers were essential for maximizing use of capacity and speeding up handling. Constructed of aluminium, the ULD is very light but fragile and thus sustains considerable damage unless properly handled. Other types of special containers have been developed such as temperature-controlled boxes for perishable cargo, pharmaceuticals, and live animal stalls.

The Boeing 747-100, the first jumbo jet, took off on its maiden flight from Seattle on 9 February 1969. The B747 was first designed for the US Air Force as a military freighter, but as Lockheed won the contract for what became the C5-Galaxy, Boeing went on to concentrate on developing the B747 as a commercial passenger and cargo aircraft which, in its successive versions, has flown the world for 45 years.

A freighter version with a larger side door and a nose-loading capability came in with the B747-200 series. Between 1970 and 1991 Boeing built 476 aircraft, including the improved B747-200 and B747-300 versions. One interesting variant was the 747 Combi or 747M for main deck. This was the perfect aircraft for countries that wanted the operating economics of the

FIGURE 3.2   ULDs maximize cargo capacity

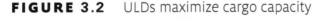

FIGURE 3.3 An early B747 freighter

747 yet did not have the passenger market to support a total passenger configuration. These aircraft were equipped with a full cargo door aft of the wing, allowing access to the main deck for palletized cargo. Two versions were offered: the seven main-deck pallet position (MDP) version, and the much larger 12 MDP versions. Carriers with a smaller home base such as KLM, China Airlines, Asiana and Air Canada were the main clients for this variant from Boeing.

A wide variety of engines and configurations were adopted during this period. Many of the passenger aircraft were subsequently converted to freighter configuration as the price of the used aircraft declined. However, operating economics of 747 converted aircraft are making this increasingly less likely in the future. This massively capital-intensive investment requires these aircraft to be in the air to make money, in every scenario. The 747 aircraft's latest variant – the B747-8F – is now in service with several freighter operators but is having a hard time justifying its existence due to the four-engine technology and high cost of fuel.

Another major economic issue is crew utilization for passenger airlines using freighters, so-called 'combination carriers'. The 747 passenger aircraft is rapidly losing favour and is being steadily withdrawn from service with most global airlines. Singapore Airlines, once one of the largest operators of the type, has completely retired its fleet in favour of the B777 and to some extent the A380. Emirates, Etihad and Qatar, the current powerhouses of the Gulf region, have never operated 747 in their own livery, other than a few ACMI leased aircraft being the only viable way to justify its use.

Other than for all-cargo operators where the flexibility and versatility of a massive aircraft like the 747-8F can be justified through cargo yields higher than for general cargo, for the most part it's increasingly the 777F that fits passenger airlines' needs for dedicated cargo operations, with the operating economics to justify its existence. The mythology of a nose door being an absolute requirement in freighters has long been debunked, as the requirement for ultra-long cargo accommodation, ie pipes that require a nose door, is less than 5 per cent of the total. Two-engine technology and substantial fuel savings over the 747, common operational requirements in maintenance and engineering, cockpit commonality with the passenger aircraft leading to reduced requirements in staff, all produce a much lower operating unit cost for the airline.

The influences in global economies, including recessions, high fuel price, wars, natural disasters and environmental considerations impact heavily on the aviation industry, which has managed to survive albeit battered but still alive. The powerhouse manufacturing countries such as China, Germany and increasingly the Indian subcontinent, coupled with efficient transport hubs such as Dubai, Korea and Frankfurt, completely changed the dynamics of the world's social and industrial landscape.

The logistics and supply chain industry has evolved to deal with this challenge and air freighting cargo is just one of many options available to shippers and consignees worldwide. This means that airline management has to understand that in today's world air cargo must be considered a core business, and be treated as such within the airline to maximize the returns. Unit costs have to be as low as possible, yet all the while delivering a quality product. Every survey of shippers and consignees reveals the same issues as being paramount: network, quality and price. For an airline to achieve this, the choice of fleet is a basic first step in meeting customer demand. Freighters can ideally complement a passenger airline's belly capacity, and when managed professionally can produce the profits needed to invest in the other aspects of cargo processing on the ground and in fleet renewal.

The major contributors

Integrators such as FedEx, UPS, DHL and TNT and many smaller operators owe their existence to their ability to control and transport documents and goods rapidly door to door, in a one-stop service. Because their entire operations are kept in-house, including for the most part the flights, they have been able to follow the progress of each package through their own tracking systems, handling facilities and ground network, meaning fewer errors, delays and losses. Integrators were the first to work closely with Customs in major destinations, and due to the volume they produced ensure on-site presence of Customs officers to expedite clearance. This competitive advantage over the traditional Customs brokerage firms allowed them to rapidly expand market share while the industry as we knew it just looked on. Another competitive coup was the 'on board courier' phenomenon where passenger 'baggage' consisting of dozens of bags was checked in at the passenger gates and flown as luggage, and then cleared at destination with the least amount of delay. Parcels quickly formed the bulk of these shipments versus mail, and again through innovation the traditional airline and forwarder partnership was cut out of the premium market.

The airlines

These express and courier methods have been instrumental in forcing the traditional air cargo industry (legacy carriers and forwarders) to change and adopt many of the same techniques and technologies to remain relevant. Techniques including tracking and tracing, product segmentation and e-freight have made shipments faster, more reliable and more transparent. Yet many legacy airlines are not investing in this technology and forwarders are not embracing the benefits; they are now paying a price. The biggest hurdle for the industry is process segmentation in the logistics chain and a lack of trust between the various components within it. Diverse interests between airlines, airports, forwarders, and ground-handling companies, Customs and government authorities lead to delays and poor service. The clients are more likely to seek a solution that 'delivers as promised', rather than one that talks about 'flown as booked'.

Electronic systems

In order to offer competitive services, airlines and forwarders, airports and Customs have had to invest in computer-based systems with a view to communicating accurately and control the cargo processes. The International Air Transport Association (IATA) and The International Air Cargo Association (TIACA) are the ones leading the way in promoting these technologies.

The introduction of Cargo Community Systems (CCS) many years ago was the first stage in this process and the advent of Electronic Data Interchange (EDI) successfully standardized methods of sending cargo messages. With the integrators' system of total freight control, the freight forwarders and airlines had to respond and offer a very similar level of service to their customers, such as door-to-door pick-up and delivery, with online tracking and tracing to back it up. To achieve this, the airlines were obliged to supply the data and an interface for the forwarder to access the network.

Acceptance of this new technology has been very slow and many companies are still resisting these computer-based systems, much to the detriment of the industry as a whole. If a solution to this dilemma is not found, the role of everyone in this business who is not on board will be relegated to that of a provider of generic services against the lowest prices amongst many. Profits will not be there to reinvest in the business, and the circle of decline will continue.

The air freight market today

Since 2008 air cargo has suffered along with the world's economies, as one economic crisis after another changed forever the way we do business. The first fact we must realize is that while air cargo stagnated or declined, the world seemed to embrace vacation travel as never before and the world's passenger fleet has grown exponentially. Initially business travel declined, but in the first quarter of 2014 signs were that this is rebounding as well. giving a much-needed boost to the airlines' bottom line. Each year most airlines have double-digit passenger growth as online booking and searches for low-cost alternatives became available for the consumer. While Europe and the Americas faced air cargo decline as consumers looked for the lowest-cost provider, emerging economies such as Asia, parts of Africa, the Gulf region and South America were still growing.

Wide-body aircraft are increasingly efficient, and can carry cargo loads in their bellies never imagined in the past. A recent study shows over 2,400 wide-body aircraft on order (excluding unnamed clients) with 864 of those being delivered in Asia, 596 in the Gulf Region, 430 in Europe and 397 in the Americas. This is in addition to the massive fleets of 777/787 and A330 that ply the skies today, and will for the most part find a second home when the newer aircraft are delivered. Table 3.1, included here courtesy of Cargo Facts, shows the effect of this. Another analysis of the effect this will have on wide body alone is shown in Table 3.2, broken down by aircraft type and with average payloads in full freighter equivalents.

The conclusion that must be drawn by airline and logistics managers around the globe is that we are facing at least a decade where cargo capacity is likely to exceed demand unless something is done to stimulate new business. The yields from cargo will not return to a level where all cargo aircraft are profitable unless this is done.

TABLE 3.1   Aircraft on order, March 2014

Region	Narrow body		Wide body		Total
	Quantity	% of total	Quantity	% of total	
North America	1,968	86.8	299	13.2	2,267
South America	546	84.7	99	15.3	645
Europe	1,687	79.7	431	20.3	2,118
Africa	110	58.5	78	41.5	188
Middle East	350	37.0	596	63.0	946
Asia Pacific	2,474	74.1	864	25.9	3,338
Total	**7,135**	**75.1**	**2,367**	**24.9**	**9,502**
Current fleet	13,040	73.9	4,610	26.1	17,650
Order as % of current fleet	54.7		51.3		53.8
Freighters in current fleet	604		958		1562
Freighters as % of fleet	4.6		20.8		8.8
Freighters on order			136	5.7	

SOURCE: CAPA

TABLE 3.2   Wide-body aircraft fleets

Wide-body Passenger Aircraft Summary					
	Ordered	Delivered	Backlog	Cargo payload (tonnes)	
Boeing				Per a/c	In Backlog
747-8I	42	9	33	15	495
777-300ER	721	458	263	26	6,838
777X	66	0	66	28	1,848
787	1,031	118	913	15	13,695
Subtotal	**1,860**	**585**	**1,275**	**Subtotal**	**22,876**
Airbus					
A330	1,274	1,030	244	15	3,660
A350	814	0	814	22	17,908
A380	304	123	181	15	2,715
Subtotal	**2,392**	**1,153**	**1,239**	**Subtotal**	**24,283**
Total	**4,252**	**1,738**	**2,514**		

SOURCE: Courtesy Cargo Facts

All-cargo operators

Against this backdrop, and with the wind-down in the US military use of civilian service providers of freighters (the Civil Reserve Air Fleet – CRAF) we have seen many casualties in the all-cargo market, especially in the United States. Names such as Evergreen Aviation and World Airways have disappeared and the remaining ACMI service providers have had to completely revise their business case to survive. What is relevant is that there is a definite need for some of these carriers; the only question is who that will be.

Based on the client's demands for network, quality and price, in that order, it would seem logical that all cargo airlines seek that scale and market attractiveness by either a tactical or strategic alliance with a passenger airline. Combining both independent carriers' strengths into one product offering may be the only choice going forward.

Most ACMI providers now are either restricting their product offering to CMI for integrators, eg Southern Air, or offering a mixed product portfolio that includes ACMI, dry lease, scheduled commercial flights and CMI only, like Atlas. Kalitta Aviation is following the same route, having been an exclusive ACMI provider to airlines and the US military, and has recently announced commercial services by 747F between the United States and the Netherlands. Only time will tell if it can compete effectively in today's market, and what niche products it will develop to sustain operations on this highly competitive route.

The remaining all-cargo operators of consequence such as Cargolux, Nippon Cargo Airlines (NCA) and AirBridgeCargo (ABC) continue to struggle as demand remains flat; yield and profit are not at the level required to sustain operations and growth. This dilemma is forcing these carriers to look at routes and products that are either underserved by passenger or combination carriers that operate freighters, or find products where main-deck capacity is an absolute necessity.

As previously mentioned the number-one requirement in numerous surveys of shippers and consignees is network – one carrier for the entire journey – followed by quality and price. Very often this network requirement is just not there in an all-cargo airline, or it cannot match that of a combination carrier (operating passenger and freighter aircraft); usually this leads to price erosion for the freighter operator to gain traffic share. Full details of the world freighter fleet may be downloaded as a pdf at **http://www.koganpage.com/product/aviation-logistics-9780749472702** (Source: thanks to *Air Cargo News*).

Combination carriers

Many of the global airlines are defined as combination carriers: airlines that operate a mixed fleet of passenger and cargo aircraft. In the past this included many US-based airlines such as American, Northwest, United and Air Canada, but they quickly dropped freighter operations as deregulation brought consolidation, and the integrators took over the higher-yielding traffic.

It was Europe that was the powerhouse in this sector, led for the most part by KLM, Lufthansa and Air France. Notable freighter operators also included British Airways, SAS, Swissair and Sabena. Slowly over the past decades major operators in Europe and the US shunned freighters, and today only Lufthansa can be said to be totally committed to the model.

Emirates: A combination carrier using passenger and freighters to maximum potential

Like other Gulf operators such as Qatar and Etihad, Emirates has a massive investment in young wide-body passenger aircraft, and also operates freighters with, for the most part, a job to 'keep the bellies full'. Here are the comments of Hiran Perera, Senior Vice President and Freighter Manager of Emirates Sky Cargo:

The cargo carrying capability of the Boeing 777-300ER is unsurpassed by any other wide-bodied passenger aircraft currently in operation. The aircraft has excellent weight and volume capability. Typical maximum range is around 10–11 hours and on such missions even with a full load of passengers with average baggage, a cargo payload of 20–22 tons can be achieved subject to the density of the freight. On missions beyond 11 hours the payload starts to drop. Emirates have uplifted a record 54 tons on a flight from KHI to DXB and have achieved cargo loads of 20–25 tons on typical routes. To put this in perspective, this is what a Boeing 737 freighter would uplift. So the cargo carrying potential of this airplane is incredible and provides an operator a significant secondary income stream.

The Boeing 777F freighter first entered service in 2009 right in the middle of the economic crisis. However, operators soon realized the potential of this aircraft even during slow economic times. The aircraft offers the lowest trip cost of any large wide-bodied freighter in service today. In an industry where directional loads are the norm, low trip cost and the excellent fuel burn of the 777F provide exceptional operating economics. While the aircraft does not have nose cargo door capability as in a 747-production freighter, the side cargo door is the widest in service. The internal contours are more limiting than a 747, but given the right density mix, a maximum payload of 102 tons net is achievable.

One disadvantage compared with the 747F is the limitation of carrying long heavy cargo as well as single pieces exceeding approximately 20 tons where the 747 has much better floor loading capability. However, when operating economics are considered the 777F has significantly lower operating cost and unit cost than a 747F. In current economic conditions the lower payload of the 777F by around 13 tons is a much lower-risk proposition as well. On the whole the 777F is the freighter of the 21st century and this is confirmed by the Boeing order book for the type.

FIGURE 3.4   Boeing 777

The benefits of the 777F as described by Hiran are clear, but as the 747 all-passenger version is being phased out by the majority of the current operators, there are other major advantages of the 777F in crew utilization, maintenance, engineering and other commonalities and this adds to the very positive operating economics of this type. Qatar, for example, achieves the same benefits from the 777F and also the A330F due to the many passenger variants of the type in its fleet.

Aircraft, Crew, Maintenance, Insurance (ACMI)

The conundrum for combination carriers will be how to source large, wide-body freighters when the market demand, product mix or economics show that a profitable operation is possible. This can be the niche that ACMI operators such as Atlas Air or Kalitta of the United States can fill. The issue that will be the biggest challenge for these operators will be to deliver a product that has a low enough unit cost for the contracting airline to be attractive. Other elements can play a factor in favour of ACMI like traffic rights issues, filling a short-term need for capacity on a seasonal or incident basis, but it will remain a hard sell going forward. Smaller or mid-sized freighters, much favoured by the integrators, should remain a viable business case provided further consolidation does not take place.

Large heavy lift aircraft

The market for large heavy lift and versatile aircraft has long been dominated by the Antonov design bureau flagship, the AN 124. Originally constructed as a platform that the Soviet Union wanted to transport mobile missile launchers, the end of the Cold War and newer technology meant these aircraft were no longer required for their original mission. Designed in the Ukraine, built in both the Antonov plant in Kiev and the Russian factory in Ulyanovsk, the aircraft went on to commercial success mostly as a result of the hard work of Alexei Isaikin, the current chairman of Volga Dnepr Group of Russia. He recognized the commercial possibilities of the aircraft especially for industrial project work, and over the past 20 years built Volga Dnepr into a near monopoly for this type of airlift. The partnership between Antonov Airlines and Ruslan International, based in Leipzig Germany, is one of the few air cargo alliances that have proved successful.

Originally designed as the AN124-100, later versions were modified and upgraded to the AN124-150 capable of carrying up to 150 metric tonnes on

FIGURE 3.5 Loading heavy outsize shipment

its roll-on-roll-off body. It is a four-engine aircraft, requiring a crew of six to operate it in the cockpit. One larger example was built, the AN 225, originally designed to carry the Soviet Union's version of the space shuttle on its back. This giant of the air can transport up to 250 metric tonnes in its cavernous main-deck holds. The aircraft holds a world record for the largest single piece transported at close to 190 metric tonnes. The aircraft languished on the ground for many years before entering commercial service in the early 2000s as part of the Antonov airlines group.

While versatile, unique and certainly capable of some missions that are impossible for Western-built aircraft, the technology employed is vastly outdated and extremely expensive to operate. As a consequence this aircraft is utilized for the missions it was designed for – unique air cargo – and could never be commercially viable for general air freight use. Commercial variants of various Western-built military aircraft such as the Lockheed C-130, Boeing C-17 and the smaller Embraer KC-390 have been touted as potential competitors in the roll-on-roll-off category, but so far the Ukrainian variants remain the dominant player.

Conclusions

We have tried to highlight, through history and the present, how the technological and economic factors that are for the most part not under the control of individual airlines are constantly challenging the business of air cargo. The market has grown and prospered over the years and matured to one that must be addressed with caution, and with management skills that demand the best we can be.

Airlines will have to invest in training and learning. They will have to make air cargo and logistics an attractive career choice, not a transitional position to move on to other posts in the airline, a career where dedicated experienced professionals are available to cope with what is to come.

The slow acceptance of IT tools that could revolutionize the way we do business, the constant turnover in senior management, the lack of innovative and creative marketing and product development can be solely laid on the shoulders of the current leadership. This must change if air cargo is to grow in step with the massive capacity increases and emergence of a wealthier global middle class who will be there to purchase the goods only air cargo can deliver. Only by making air cargo a core business in every airline, a position it deserves, will this change.

We would like to give the last word to Joseph (Joe) Czyzyk, CEO and founder of the Mercury Group in the United States, a true legend in the business and someone who knows. From an interview he gave and with Joe's permission, here are his thoughts:

Joe Czyzyk

Fred Smith saying that 'the halcyon days of air cargo are over' tells me that although he is the greatest, he hasn't got this one quite right (regarding the speech of Fred Smith, founder of Fed Ex at a recent IATA conference). Smith appears to have a very short- to medium-range outlook that is understandable in his business, but his medium to long-term range outlook for air cargo will not materialize as he thinks. The truth is that the world is going to experience another 1 billion-plus people joining the middle class in the next decade from the emerging nations. And what is the definition of someone from the middle class? It is someone who not only subsists, but has a few bucks to purchase an iPad, get on an airplane, and in the larger picture be someone who will want stuff shipped to them. Maybe in the short term air cargo is taking a hit whilst experiencing a bit of flattening out but given the realities of our global future, I think that air cargo will as an industry keep moving on and will grow into an even greater business.

In the early 1970s when the first B747F air cargo freighters were introduced on non-stop transatlantic and trans-Pacific flights, a barrel of oil was at US$12, the amortization or depreciation for a 747F was US$250,000 per month, fully allocated operating cost were approx. US$5,000 per hour, the cost of warehouse and ramp labour was US$5 per hour, and the air cargo rates were between US$1.50 and US$2.00 per kg in either direction for a transatlantic flight. Today, all of those costs have tripled, quadrupled, and fuel has multiplied eight times, but only one of those numbers has remained the same and in many cases has even decreased. Of course, that's the rate per kilogram without even adjusting the present day value of money. So it's natural that so many airlines, with a few exceptions, are looking to reduce or completely eliminate their freighter fleets.

While more than half of the air cargo in the world is flown in the bellies of passenger aircraft and that percentage will continue to grow over the decades, there will be less and less incentive for combination carriers to artificially adjust their tariffs to support their freighter fleets. It will be more accretive for them to park their freighters, as many have already done. Another one of our customers with a full passenger load flew its A380 nonstop to Dubai and carried more than 18 tons of cargo in their belly while their triple seven (777) carried 25 tons. It's obvious that air cargo pricing will become more and more influenced by passenger carriers. The operating costs of a passenger carrier on a ton/kilometre basis will remain more flexible, profitable, and their reliability and frequency will continue to outpace the all-cargo carriers.

So what's the future of the freighter aircraft?

There will always be a need, but survival and profitability will require higher pricing, eg for shipments exceeding 2.4 meters in height, very heavy shipments, charter work, government, aerospace, and specialized shipments, but certainly fewer of them flying on scheduled routes, and I suspect that Boeing will eventually shut down its freighter manufacturing lines over the next decade, as the demand decreases.

I predict that, except for the integrated package delivery carriers, there will be no growth and most probably a progressive reduction of freighter operations from Los Angeles (LAX), simultaneous with international tonnage increasing over the next decade. Today in our business, where my company provides warehousing services for international airlines, we are analysing that eventuality and its impact on our business. More and more of our systems are becoming geared towards accommodating the cargo preparation, loading and delivery systems for passenger flights.

Let's face it, more and more people are travelling by air and as the next billion earth inhabitants (as mentioned earlier) join the middle class over the next decade, many of them will want to fly and that sheer growing demand for passenger travel will provide a tremendous abundance of additional air cargo capacity without adding many more freighters. Of course my comments need a 'safe harbour' statement, and just as Fred Smith pointed out in his keynote remarks at WCS, because all predictions are theory and certain future events such as simple acts of aviation terrorism or a dramatic reduction in the price of jet fuel can easily invalidate these predictions.

Joe's words accurately sum up what the industry challenges will be. Do not be fooled and think this is a United States-only phenomenon because Joe is based there – his company is global. It is our responsibility in air cargo to make sure the management and staff of airlines, logistics companies and all the associations and government authorities that are needed to make it work are on the right track to ensure its survival as the premier transportation mode, and one that is always profitable for its investors. We need to invest in training and knowledge transfer to the young leaders of today and show them what an exciting business this can be, when managed properly.

Airport connections

04

The world's 8,707 ICAO-designated airports form the link for not only passengers but also import and export cargo carried on flights serving any airport and its market. Most of these airports are for local traffic only and have little or no cargo except for postal business. It is difficult to define airports where cargo is important as in some agricultural areas exporting fresh produce, the airport will play a larger role than normal. This chapter provides a brief overview of the airport sector.

All airports are in place to connect passengers, mail and air cargo to local markets and services. They may be the very large global hubs, such as Dubai, Paris or Atlanta, but other regional airports such as Liège in Belgium or East Midlands in the United Kingdom are also significant for cargo traffic. They may be integrator stations with special sorting facilities, dedicated freighter hubs or perishables centres. In the face of high costs and the trend of using passenger aircraft bellies for cargo, some airports are finding life increasingly difficult. In the case of Manston in Kent, England, the volumes of cargo traffic did not generate sufficient revenue and it was forced to close.

Globalization

Some airports have opened the door for multimodal logistics and distribution centres, assembly and repairs, often within duty free zones. Globalization has introduced the concept of multi-source manufacturing with products such as capital goods and electronics being supplied by air cargo transportation to maintain assembly lines, or just-in-time e-tailing, with components from different sources. Airports play an important role in maintaining the global supply chain.

The growth of airports and ground services came about as a result of pressure from airlines, but they quickly realized the potential profits to be made. Back in the early days, the lack of suitable safe navigation aids and ground facilities limited aviation's progress. European carriers were quicker

FIGURE 4.1   Schiphol airport top cargo hub

than their US counterparts in setting up ground and navigation facilities, necessary for passengers, mail or freight traffic. Nowadays, it is rarely viable to fly cargo within a country, so around 80 per cent of all internal cargo between airports in Europe and the United States goes by road with some by rail.

For air cargo operators, it is the minimum time spent on the ground plus road links that are important in gaining access to local or transit markets. Cargo operations require warehouses and cool rooms, health controls and Customs with easy access to the aircraft. High levels of security are obligatory, with trained handling staff. Their job is to build or break down pallets as efficiently and quickly as possible. Handling companies must invest in modern computer systems, warehouse equipment and warehousing facilities (see Chapter 5).

Despite the congestion on the roads, especially in Europe, most road feeder services (RFS) move during the night, thus having less impact on traffic congestion. Clearly in less developed countries, airports are more basic and the provision of facilities such as cool storage is a top priority, especially when the main exports are perishable goods. In many cases retail chains may operate dedicated farms and handling facilities within a specific country to ensure the integrity of their produce.

Environmental pressures

All-night, 24-hour operation is becoming rarer as more airports have night restrictions placed upon them. Freighters and express traffic fly mostly at night when possible and many of the express operators have use of 24-hour airports, but today the airlines have to plan their schedules very carefully. Recently Frankfurt airport, the main freighter centre for Lufthansa Cargo, was forced by the authorities to impose a night curfew, causing problems for the airline. The airline was able to rearrange its flight schedule.

An airport is called a hub when airlines operate an interchange of flights with a high proportion of both passengers and cargo being in transit. This is an efficient way of maximizing aircraft capacity and investment of both airlines and airports. A perfect example of this would be Dubai, the main hub for Emirates airlines, which operates a global network. Flights arriving or departing from international destinations enter the hub where both passengers and cargo can be repositioned on flights for other destinations. A massive investment in new airport facilities and passenger comfort attracts business, making the airport profitable.

TABLE 4.1 World's leading cargo airports, 2013

		Tonnage (approx, million tons)
1	Hong Kong	4.6
2	Memphis	4.56
3	Shanghai	3.23
4	Incheon	2.72
5	Dubai	2.68
6	Louisville	2.44
7	Frankfurt	2.31
8	Paris CDG	2.28
9	Tokyo	2.23
10	Miami	2.14
11	Singapore	2.08
12	Beijing	2.03
13	Los Angeles	1.93
14	Taipei	1.73
15	Amsterdam	1.73
16	London HR	1.67
17	Guangzhou	1.44
18	New York JFK	1.43
19	Bangkok	1.36
20	Chicago	1.35

Airport types

Airports can be mostly described as:

- *International hubs,* where many different carriers operate for both passenger and cargo. Examples are London, New York, Miami and Frankfurt. Cargo may reach its local destination or be re-routed via another airline connection to a further destination.

- *Smaller airports* such as Munich, Mumbai, Houston and Singapore, which perform a similar role but on a smaller scale.

- *Small regional airports* such as Bristol in the United Kingdom, Bilbao in Spain or Halifax Stanfield in Canada, which are building up considerable passenger traffic where travellers are avoiding big hub airports.

- *Cargo-friendly airports,* where the air freight business is the main activity. These include Liège (Belgium), Cologne and Frankfurt-Hahn in Germany. These airports welcome cargo traffic while some of the bigger hubs do not want freighters and cargo-related activities.

Whatever the size or location, all airports must provide runways of 3,000 m, electronic navigation equipment, radar, beacons and perimeter fence security. Various international organizations, as well as national ones, such as the Federal Aviation Administration (FAA) in the United States or the Civil Aviation Authority (CAA) in the United Kingdom, control these facilities.

International hubs

All these airport hubs maintain an economic balance between passenger and cargo traffic.

Hong Kong International Airport is the busiest air cargo gateway in the world, handling over 4 million tons per year. The airport provides all the facilities and services needed by cargo operators. It was constructed well away from the city centre, which keeps all noise and emissions far away. It is one of the leading gateways for the Chinese mainland and incorporates the highest standards in equipment as well as security. Its success is due to its strategic position next to China, with direct access to factories in the Pearl River Delta. Despite its size, Hong Kong airport is planning to increase its facilities.

Miami International Airport has unrivalled cargo flights serving Latin America and the Caribbean as well as an overall total of around 90 carriers

– US, foreign and special cargo charters. The Airport's significant gains in the world's air cargo market have provided widespread economic benefits for Miami-Dade County. The Airport's trade supports more than 1,000 freight forwarders and almost 250 Customs brokers located around the airport. Traffic is expedited by a unique 'one-stop' Cargo Clearance Center, with some 300 inspectors from US Customs and Border Protection, US Fish and Wildlife Service, and US Food and Drug Administration providing a 24-hour cargo clearance operation. Other on-airport businesses include aircraft leasing, crew training facilities, and aircraft maintenance.

Miami's trade is largely with the Caribbean and Latin American countries, especially in perishables such as flowers, seafood, fruit and vegetables, plus some clothing. MIA's export cargo is comprised of computers and peripherals, machinery, medical equipment, telecommunications equipment, agricultural machinery, apparel articles and aircraft parts.

Miami Airport handles over 80 per cent of all exports from the Latin American/Caribbean region, and is ranked 10th in the world. The airport connects to markets in Europe, the Middle East and Asia as well as Australasia. Sophisticated packaging and marketing techniques, such as labelling flowers and fruit directly at the grower for specific retailers, speed the process and increase the shelf life. A total of some 2 million tons of air cargo, worth around US$61.5 million, of which around 88 per cent is international, passes through Miami. There is a road corridor linking the cargo area to the warehouse district and on to the interstate highway system, carrying over 200,000 truck movements annually.

Dubai: the original 35,000 square metre Dubai Airport's cargo facility was built at a cost of US$75 million in 1991 with a capacity for handling 150,000 tonnes. The Cargo Mega Terminal was opened in 2008 at a cost of more than US$200 million, with increased capacity of 2.5 million tonnes. Dubai Airport is served by over 125 airlines flying to more than 260 destinations worldwide. The facilities include 56 truck docks for import, export and perishable cargo, and seven docks dedicated to sea–air traffic. The storage facility has small warehouse pallets with 902 positions, regular 1,698 positions, large 1,126 positions and mini shipments 760 (single positions), as well as 18 positions for storing perishables. Dubai has rapidly developed from a largely sea–air trans-shipment base into one of the world's top passenger and cargo hubs, in parallel with the rise of Emirates airlines. Dubai itself has expanded its business and trading status but the airline's operations benefit from its unique route network.

Small and medium airports

These serve their local catchment areas for both passengers and cargo. In most cases cargo plays a minor role but is still important to the airport's bottom line. For example, Dusseldorf International Airport is situated in the North Rhine Westphalia region, traditional home to Germany's heavy industries. In recent years it has been chosen by Chinese and Japanese companies to base their European offices and is a good example of how an airport becomes an integral part of the business and social community. The whole of northern Europe is within a few hours by road.

The airport is the third-busiest passenger gateway in Germany with 70 airlines serving over 180 destinations worldwide. It serves as a secondary hub for Air Berlin and Lufthansa as well as benefiting from multiple daily flights to and from the Middle East. Main-deck freighter traffic is relatively small, but belly-hold cargo represents over 100,000 tons of air cargo capacity a year.

The airport has become a busy hub connected to a growing number of intercontinental destinations, making it increasingly important for the big forwarders and logistics companies. Its ready access to a wide range of lower-deck capacity, together with an independent trucking network based in a high potential catchment area is stimulating Dusseldorf's further cargo growth. (Source: DUS Cargo)

Specialist cargo airports

There are many airports around the world where cargo plays a more important role than passenger traffic. The airport may have space for large-scale seasonal charter operations, for example the New Beaujolais traffic at Chateauroux in France, and seasonal produce imports at Ostend (Belgium). Each one of these airports has marginal low-cost airline traffic and they are all situated some distance from major passenger destinations. They are mostly open at night and can all handle large freighter aircraft such as an AN-124 or a B747F. Thanks to an absence of congestion they are capable of achieving a fast turnaround. As cargo traffic swings more than ever to passenger belly-hold, some cargo airports are experiencing difficulties but others may be able to increase their integrator and low-cost airline business.

Integrators

Because of the need for speed and freedom to fly at night, the main integrators, such as FedEx, DHL and UPS, have developed their own hubs where only cargo is handled. For example, FedEx has a long established hub at Paris CDG, UPS at Cologne and DHL at Leipzig. In the United States, FedEx Express's Memphis 'Superhub' contains over 300 miles of linked conveyor belts which comprise a digital sorting and processing system for domestic and international small packages trans-shipped through the facility. The hub handles an average of about 3.3 million packages per day and employs more than 8,000 workers during the night shift. FedEx Express began operations at Memphis in 1973 with a single Dassault Falcon 20 Jet and is now the world's largest air cargo carrier and the largest of the FedEx subsidiary companies.

Summary

In summary, modern airports around the world have become an essential factor in most countries' economies. Passenger traffic combines with freight, express and mail plus the expansion of aviation-related businesses around the airport perimeter, to create modern export-led business communities within the local, regional and national economy. In the world of the global supply chain, these airports are key performance links for businesses.

Cargo handling agents – the impact of IT

05

Early days

We all take air travel for granted these days. Simply log onto the internet, select the route and not only can we book the flight, pay for it, choose our seats, book a special meal and print the boarding pass but we can also compare the offers from the different airlines so we know we are getting a good deal. Then we add hotels, car hire and give advance immigration information so hopefully we speed through the formalities of air travel.

Wind the clock back 50 years or so to 1960 and it was a very different situation. The travel agent was king. Airline reservations were organized using shoeboxes and blackboards. A single price existed for each class of travel between two airports. Yield management was non-existent.

If you wanted to book a flight from Heathrow to Paris, say, you would go to a travel agent first. The agent would ask you which dates you wished to fly on and by looking up in a very thick book (ABC) could price the ticket. If you wanted to go ahead, the agent then had to ring the airline to find out availability. For BEA, this meant calling the reservations unit, which was in a very large room with all the walls covered in blackboards with each flight number and date on them and the current number of seats available in each class. If you wanted to book the flight an instruction was given to the reservation agent who climbed up the ladder to wipe out the number chalked on the blackboard and reduce it by one. This process was then repeated for the return journey. Your details were then written on two pieces of card, one for each leg of the journey, and these were placed into the relevant shoebox for that flight. These were called Passenger Name Records (PNR), a term that remains today in the computer systems.

On the day before departure, the shoebox for the Paris–London leg was flown out to Paris so it was available for check-in next day. (So if you wanted to book on today's flight, the reservations unit had to ring Paris, as the inventory was in the shoebox there.) On the day of departure all the shoeboxes for the flights departing from Heathrow were taken to the airport for check-in. Frequent inconsistencies in the data held led to reduced service levels and major problems with capacity control.

Airlines at the start of computer technology

1956 – IBM/AA Saber

Computers really started to become commonplace in businesses during the 1950s. Banks led the way, but airlines were very quick to seize on the potential to revolutionize their business by adopting this technology. In 1956, a lunch-time meeting between the CEOs of American Airlines and IBM led to the first passenger reservations system – SABER (Semi-Automatic Business Environment Research), which went live in 1964. The initial aim was to automate the process from reservation through to check-in but the technology available at the time simply was not up to the job and it would take another 20 years before this became a reality. The initial SABER system had 7.2 million characters of memory and disc storage for 800 million characters (800MB) of data. How things have changed.

1964 – IBM 360 series, PARS

By 1965 the IBM SABER project had demonstrated that real-time tele-processing was a viable solution to the airlines' reservation management process. IBM wished to capitalize on the research and development put into the SABER project that had until then been a United States-only market. IBM wanted to create a system that would be suitable for all airlines. This opportunity arrived when IBM came out with the IBM360 series of computers: they created a mini revolution in the mainframe market, setting a standard that lasted a very long time. By utilizing special features in the operating system, IBM created a new version of its airline system called PARS (Programmed Airline Reservation System). The lead customer for PARS was Eastern Airlines, which wished to compete with the SABER-equipped American, Delta and Pan Am airlines.

1965 – IBM and BOAC, IPARS

It would take until 1970/71 for most of the top 10 trunk carriers in the United States to implement computer reservation systems, with nine using the IBM PARS system and one (Northwest), using Univac. The drawback was that these systems were still very United States-specific, so IBM cooperated with BOAC to create an international version: IPARS. BOAC became the first European carrier to adopt a computer reservations system that included reservations, passenger name records, capacity control and inter-airline messaging. This was very important in Europe; for example, 60 per cent of BEA's reservations actually came from other airlines. Inter-airline messages were based on an IATA standard called AIRIMP; they were no more than formatted telexes sent over the airline-owned SITA network. The BOAC system was named BOADICEA.

Beacon was British European Airways' computer online network, initially developed in 1963–7 to provide a full-scale passenger reservations service. Subsequently, the hardware was upgraded, and further applications added on an integrated basis. Later, following the merger with BOAC to form British Airways, these services were progressively taken over by Beacon's old rival system BOADICEA.

1974 – Alitalia, FAST (PO4) system developed from IPARS

In 1970 IATA found to its disappointment that the airlines were tending to look for their own in-house solutions for EDP cargo systems and there was hardly any exchange of information between airlines or any other participant in the air freight chain, causing data to be retyped multiple times and delaying the processing of the freight. In 1972 it set up a study group called CART (Cargo Automation Research Team) to address the problem. In December 1973 it produced a report that was very far-sighted for the time; it would take many participants in the logistics chain 40 years to adopt the recommendations. Many of the facts stated are still true.

The report states these basic truths: the fundamental advantage of air freight is speed, and much of this (time) is being lost on the ground, in cargo agents' warehouses and airlines' cargo terminals since air freight spends 90 per cent of its time on the ground. The report concluded that the solution was to expand the use of Electronic Data Processing (EDP) throughout the industry and to augment it with a set of standard messages that could utilize the SITA network to enable the rapid and efficient exchange of data. As with the passenger business, where IATA manages the AIRIMP message standards, a new set of committees and teams now created the CARGO-IMP set of standard messages. In fact these teams were only disbanded in October 2013 with the publishing of the 'final' versions as IATA moves from CARGO-IMP to XML message structures.

In the early 1970s Alitalia's EDP department saw an opportunity to create a cargo version of the BOAC IPARS system replacing the PNR records with a CAR (Cargo Activity Record) but retaining the use of the schedules and aircraft type data tables, replacing the passenger manifest with the cargo manifest and adding the airway bill data that forms the main record. In the initial version, Unit Load Device (ULD) control was not included, nor was pricing or dangerous goods handling. It was quite a basic system that had many shortcomings including: the flight record was only open for reservations 12 days before departure and the airway bill records were only retained online for 14 days after the record had been closed (usually through delivery to the import broker or transfer to another airline). However, it was a major step forward using the same mainframes that the airlines had bought for their passenger systems; many airlines bought the system including British Airways.

1980 – BA goes live with Fast 2 Alitalia system called BA80

BA exchanged its advanced passenger departure control system (DCS) for the PO2 system which, after four years of localization to meet UK Customs requirements, etc, replaced the CALC system in 1980 as BA80. Apart from American Airlines Freight-Sabre system, the Alitalia system became the IBM standard for airlines, and with the assistance and development effort provided by SITA to create the FAST 4 version, became the dominant system in use by 50+ airlines worldwide. It is still in use.

Early 1970s – UNIVAC (Unisys) USAS Cargo

Meanwhile, UNIVAC was also notching up sales of its USAS passenger system. It followed in the footsteps of Alitalia by creating a cargo version, which was adopted by the airlines using UNIVAC (now UNISYS) technology such as Lufthansa, Air France, Qantas Northwest and Air Canada to name a few.

2014 – Legacy systems holding airlines back

The problem today is that these 'legacy' systems are still in place at the majority of the world's large airlines. The systems are written in Assembler, basically machine language using high transaction-based operating systems such as ALCS but residing on large mainframes requiring substantial operator support. Many airlines have outsourced their hosting of the systems to large IT companies, but retain the development resources in-house as these are both scarce and expensive in the marketplace. Most of these large cumbersome systems have been supplemented with additional modern add-ons such as yield management, pricing, revenue accounts and automated warehouse management. However, they still operate on fixed size data records/tables that are expensive to change, especially when you need to increase the record size due to new requirements. The cost and (more important for the airlines) the inertia involved in changing these legacy systems are holding back the pace of change in airlines so much that some are just now making the leap to new RDBMS-based solutions that are emerging from the Middle and Far East airline-focused software houses.

For an industry that depends on speed as one of its prime selling points, airlines are very conservative and relatively slow to change systems and procedures. This seems to be truer in cargo (than passenger) where technical change really hasn't happened for 30 years. There are many reasons for this, including the lower volume of transactions, the number of parties involved in the supply chain and the fact that for most passenger airlines, cargo makes up a relatively low proportion of its revenues. With historically decreasing yields, ever increasing costs (especially fuel) and being the 'poor partner', cargo department chiefs find it difficult to compete for limited investment resources available within an airline. Therefore the reasons for change often happen externally to the airline where legislation or Customs authorities dictate that change will happen.

Change factors

For the past 30 years or more, four main parties or factors have been behind the majority of change that has happened in air freight:

1 Customs authorities;
2 IATA (including Cargo 2000);
3 the impact of the integrated operator; and
4 security requirements post 9/11.

1. Customs system – UK

Up until the early 1960s cargo volumes in the UK were relatively low. As international trade by air expanded and with the launch of Boeing 707 and Douglas DC-8 freighters, volumes stated to climb rapidly. This placed a strain on Customs services, causing severe delays in clearing goods. As these sheds filled up with this backlog, airlines sought to mitigate their costs by imposing storage charges on consignments still in their sheds, causing annoyance to and objections from importers. Two people were instrumental in suggesting that the clearing of imports via a computer system should be investigated: the Collector of Customs, James Blunt, and the Head of Air France in the UK, Etienne Drayfous.

At this time, the government tended to rely on a subsidiary of the GPO (General Post Office) known as The National Data Processing Service to create computer systems, so it was to this body that the task fell of dealing with the specifications and getting agreement from all the stakeholders involved. This process was started in 1967. At that time the GPO was the provider of telephone services in the United Kingdom, in addition to the postal service. It was also actively engaged in the development of computers for commercial applications, which would lead eventually to the emergence of Syntegra as a division of the privatized company British Telecommunications Ltd and its long-running relationship with HM Customs systems. A study gave a strong indication that computers could be a solution to the problem of delays and the government gave its consent to proceed.

Computer hardware was very expensive both to buy and to run, requiring purpose-built computer rooms staffed with operators. The chosen supplier was ICL (International Computers Limited). The system envisaged a movement of data that was unprecedented for its age. Import agents would be advised of consignments arriving at the airline warehouses via the system, which involved each airline maintaining records of which agent cleared the freight for which consignee, plus it introduced abbreviations for agents (such as a three-letter code) that still exist today. Eventually all groups accepted the specification of the system and, having agreed to it, it was necessary to give it a suitable name. Customs financed the project so it chose the name LACES, the initials of the London Airport Customs Entry System.

Live testing of the system was started during 1970. Testing involved not only checking the accuracy of each transaction but also the logic behind the Customs clearances and the transmission of data to and from the airline systems. Most airline systems were on IBM technology, none were on ICL; each manufacturer of computer hardware in those days had proprietary operating systems and even low-level design criteria such as how many bits made a byte or a word. This meant that in all cases airlines had to employ the use of converters, known as 'zircon boxes', to interface with the system, creating a mini market for another UK company with technical knowledge.

The airline systems held the CAR (Cargo Activity Records) for all the consignments landed from their flights that were subjected to the clearance formalities required by HM Customs. The zircon boxes allowed the data to be passed to LACES quickly, accurately and without human intervention, showing considerable savings in time. When a consignment had been Customs 'cleared', LACES automatically updated the relative airline system with the release authority to the appropriate airline import shed and the designated agent, once more saving time. A combined release note and Customs clearance note was then printed, allowing freight to be collected.

The system included a program to select, at random, a percentage of consignments for physical examination and a hold notice was automatically served on the airline systems until a Customs officer was available to make the examination. The agent and the airline imports department were advised of this action on the visual display unit (VDU) on which the entry data had been input and also on the airline inventory system, prohibiting delivery to the agent until examination had taken place.

There was no doubt about the time-saving benefit that LACES would provide; there was, however, the question of cost. The hardware alone would cost millions of pounds and the development of the software would cost a multiple of that so it's not surprising that cost was at the forefront of the agent's mind. Although Customs were pressed on numerous occasions, this information was not obtained until the summer of 1971 when the first airline was due to be connected to the system. This took place at the end of August. The entire cost of LACES was borne by the Treasury in the name of HM Customs and it therefore fell to it to ascertain the realistic price per year to each user, to recoup the start-up cost and the annual running cost. All agents were shocked when the price was announced, at a little over £6,000 for each VDU per year. Very few agents were willing or able to pay this much.

Why were the costs so high? Well, there was the cost of the VDU itself plus the cost of the landline to the mainframe. It was a green screen system connected over a standard telephone line that probably worked at 2,400 kb/sec (Baud) plus there were all the development and hardware costs and the third-party hosting costs of the data centre. Fortunately, the GPO, which created the system, also ran the telephone system otherwise costs could have been much higher.

One mitigating factor was that the system had been designed so that the agent user of each terminal was identified by a key (known as a Badge). The Badge code identified the user (agent) so that one VDU could be shared by many agents, each with their own Badge codes. This meant that several agents collaborated together and in fact led to many mergers. Each agent to whom the Badge had been issued by HM Customs could use the system to ascertain if any consignments had arrived for its customers.

A terminal was rented by an agent for an annual fee and was allowed more than one Badge. Due to this, the renting agent could provide other, smaller, agents with access to the terminal in order to clear their traffic. Such agents paid a fee for this access to the terminal, either an annual or monthly amount, or per-clearance. A set up such as this allowed smaller agents use of the terminal at minimal cost, while the hosting agent was able to offset its larger costs (the annual fee) through the payments received from smaller agents.

When Britain entered the Common Market or EEC (the European Economic Community) in 1973 it brought in a raft of new requirements that HM Customs was obliged to meet. LACES was modified to cope with many of these requirements, but advances in computer technology meant that LACES was now considered outdated and the ICL-based environment in which it operated obsolete.

It was British Telecom (BT), formed in 1980 and now responsible for all of the GPO's telecommunications functions and business, that HM Customs looked to when it explored the possibility of a new purpose-built operating system. The proposed system was to fully incorporate all the features and functions required by HM Customs, build on the experience gained with LACES, include an EDI (Electronic Data Interchange) and be used to process entries that were transmitted to the system by agents and airlines that had generated them on their own computers. Delays in the design and construction of this system meant that in 1981 little of note had been achieved. That well known 'late development' phrase was in regular use as additional unplanned features had to be added to LACES so that the older system could interface with a system known as DEPS (Departmental Entry Processing System).

DEPS had been designed and controlled by HM Customs and Excise (HMCE) to comply with the law regarding the importation of goods into the UK, and also to further improve the speed and reliability of inward cargo clearance. When an agent logged on to DEPS it was able to enter waybill details simply and without the complicated commands that were previously required – these commands had been very easy to get wrong and required extensive operator training. DEPS would check every item of the entry input including tariff description, allocation of freight charges, foreign currency conversions, Value Added Tax and Duty calculations.

Electronic payments were now possible as the system maintained a credit status for each agent, and as long as sufficient credit or funds had been lodged with HMCE, the agent's credit account would be automatically debited with whatever fees or duties were due on consignments. DEPS would then allocate each shipment to the relevant clearance route for that shipment:

- Route Ones – must be held for examination of the hard copy of the documents which the agent would lodge with Customs. DEPS issued a hold message to the airline prohibiting release of the physical freight until this action had been performed and a release note printed.

- Route Twos – required for physical examination; DEPS put the release on hold until that examination had been satisfactorily completed.

- Route Threes – were granted immediate release subject to a one-hour delay to enable a Customs officer to intervene if he or she so wished.

The UK had led the way in the introduction of automated Customs systems and this enabled most clearances to be completed in a few hours instead of three or four days, giving the UK an edge over its European neighbours. The value to the UK international trading community was therefore enormous and its logical efficiency was recognized by many of the country's foreign trading partners who sent representatives to see how it was done. Without exception they were astonished at the level of efficiency achieved.

The impact of changes in law and import tariffs has had, and always will have, a sizeable impact on the trading community, and HMCE recognized this. Many committees were set up and some still exist (in modified form) as change comes faster and from many directions.

When looking to update or replace LACES, the main committee was normally chaired by HMCE and attended by agents, airlines and BT. The Technical Committee was comprised of the same representatives but was chaired by BT. The Airline Steering Committee (ASC) was responsible for airline requirements while the National Air Forwarding Division of the Institute of Freight Forwarders, now known as the British International Freight Association (BIFA) worked on behalf of agents' interests. It was these committees that agreed on a replacement for LACES and approved a new updated interim system known as ACP80 (Air Cargo Processing 1980s), run by BT. The ACP80 system was LACES plus several additional facilities, which accessed HM Customs and airlines via the VDU.

ACP80 worked exceedingly well during this period, but computer technology was again rapidly improving and updating, with relational databases becoming the standard rather than the table-based systems then in place (and utilized by ACP80). It was suggested therefore that an entirely new system should be developed to work with a new independent Customs system to be known as CHIEF. Software development didn't always run smoothly and the UK experienced one almighty failure. A division of British Airways named Travicom was given the task of producing the new system (UKAS). It was extensively tested for the correct operation of the trade functions but when it was eventually released to the users, it crashed spectacularly as the new technology simply could not cope with the throughput required of it. Indeed, I remember dealing with KLM at the time: it had introduced a new program that ran daily but took 26 hours to process! The ability to tune programs for efficient code became an absolute necessity. Needless to say the trade community in the UK fell back on BT to produce a solution. BT updated ACP80 to cope with the requirements of the time and, when this interim system was introduced, it was named ACP90.

ACP90's primary function was to interface with DEPS, but both these mainframe-based systems were becoming outdated and the environment in which it was coded made it both expensive and difficult to maintain. Distributed processing was being introduced along with new network protocols, so many of the functions that resided in ACP80/90 were now to be designed for PCs. A new system was required.

The new forwarders system would be known as ASM2000 while any airlines/handling agents that did not modify their own systems would use a system called ABS. The system to connect to CHIEF (which had finally been introduced after many delays) was called CCS-UK (Cargo Community System) and would be managed on behalf of the community by BT. It would retain many of the features of the old LACES system including the funding through charging for Badge codes and transaction fees, but the old VDUs would be replaced by PCs connected via an X25 network.

ASM2000 was designed, for the first time, with input from the one of the agent's own technicians. Computer expert Bill White was engaged to head the ASM team's involvement in this new system and his knowledge and dedication helped ensure that the agent's new system was the best that it could be. ASM still exists today with its SEQUOIA software performing the same tasks as before but encompassing all the modern requirements except e-freight.

ACP90 had also included a bureau system for those airlines operating their own sheds at LHR or for handling agents that did not have their own system. When CHIEF was being developed, it was realized that the 20 or so companies using the bureau would have no choice but to create a replacement system. Fortunately, one of those affected, Cargo Handling Technologies, had a very astute manager in Luthier Brazier who managed to convince 20 like-minded companies to share the costs of developing a replacement and funding the contract with BT to build it. Airports Bureau Systems Ltd (ABS) was born in 1993 and was responsible for managing the contract with BT. The ABS2000 system was installed all over the UK and provided those functions required by a GHA (General Handling Agent). Today ABS is about to launch its new product ABS5 in three continents with over 30 users including the major handling companies of WFS, Swissport, Dnata and Servisair.

Through the foresight of those early computer pioneers that created LACES, the foundations were laid for the current CCS-UK system, which is totally paperless for those that participate in it. The system is overseen by a user group made up of directors from ASM, ABS and the representatives from the Airline Consultative Committee, so the main three industries of airlines, forwarders and handling agents are able to influence developments and tariffs.

For those airlines that operated into the UK during the past 40 years, the paperless process has provided them with the ability to adopt all the messages (UNEDIFACT) for Customs and to exchange data with the other parties in the logistics pipeline. Although these could be provided by a third party, many chose to integrate these requirements into their own systems and the basis for e-freight could be said to have started with LACES, which is why it was so significant a change.

Today HM Customs is starting to define the system that will replace CHIEF in 2018. The X25 network has been replaced with an internet-based VPN and BT is still managing CCS-UK. While many other countries have now adopted many of its features, not one other country has quite matched the efficiency of the UK system.

2. IATA

In the 1970s IATA concluded that it took six or seven days on average to move a piece of freight. To date the industry has so far managed to shave off a few hours from that timescale. A lack of data exchange is still the single most important reason for lack of progress and this is why the e-freight project receives so much attention from IATA. It's also no surprise to find that many of the cargo officials in IATA either came from the UK market (especially British Airways) or had experience of it. The model that IATA is trying to move to closely echoes the features existing in CCS-UK.

FIGURE 5.1 CCS-UK flowchart

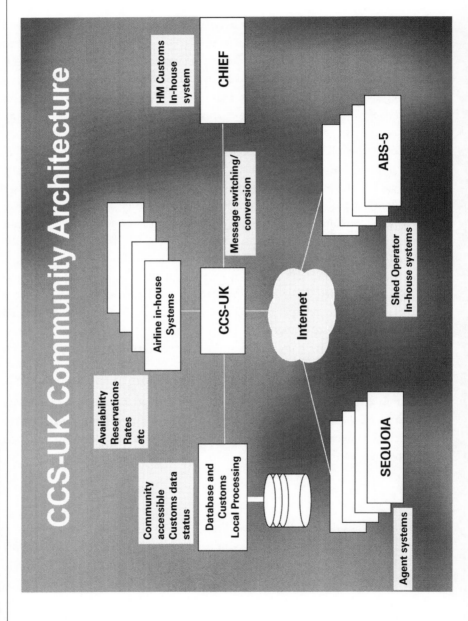

IATA grew up as the governing body of air travel, but has transformed itself into an industry champion for change and a guardian of industry-wide standards and procedures, for example dangerous goods handling. Its current focus (and for the last five years at least) has been to introduce e-AWB and e-freight into the air cargo industry. Recently, Des Vertannes, global head of cargo at IATA, said: 'Generally we need to move the goalposts. Customers are paying for a premium service but they are not getting one. It's incumbent on the industry to revolutionize the process.' IATA's aim is to raise quality and speed of delivery.

The industry needs to cut 48 hours off the average end-to-end time of a consignment by the end of this decade. The problem is that targets for IATA e-freight keep slipping. At the 2010 Air Cargo Forum, the expectation was that the whole cargo industry would be paperless by 2014, but IATA reset its target as 22 per cent of feasible shipments by the end of 2014 and it fell very short of that.

When asked for the reasons for the slippage, IATA quotes the sluggish uptake of paperless Customs clearances in several key countries. Two notable examples are India and China, which have signed the 1999 Montreal Convention that makes paperless carriage possible but still insist on physical documents for Customs clearances. It also recognizes that six consecutive years of market stagnation have meant that airline cargo departments have reduced scope to invest in the IT systems required to support e-freight.

This explains the slow take-up, but the real stopper is answering the question 'What's in it for us?' for every part of the pipeline. One can see how an airline can benefit from removing the management of paper, and a GHA will be forced to accept e-freight because the airlines say so. The real issue is what's in it for the agent and shipper. For the agent, it's all about reducing the time taken for the truck driver to deliver or pick up at the airline's warehouse. Data entry takes a long time but IATA completely misses the point that the receiving facility needs to know what's on the truck before it arrives. Just having the waybill data electronically is not enough: receivers need the truck manifest as well or a pick-up list for imports.

The good news is that in 2014 there were real signs that airlines and the larger forwarders were really getting to grips with e-freight, and speed of adoption is increasing. It is still limited as the procedures defined by IATA do not cover those procedures in the warehouse: this is left to the individual operators, but some are moving to electronic procedures faster than others.

3. Integrated operators

In 1973 Federal Express began door-to-door deliveries within the United States with a fleet of Falcon executive jets converted to carry cargo. Its pick-up and delivery service was limited at the start but it had one major advantage from day one: it had its own computer system covering all the steps from pick-up to delivery. In 1975 UPS finally obtained the rights to operate freely to 48 states in the United States. These two modern-day giants have been joined by DHL and TNT as the key innovators in the freight market.

The inability of the airlines to control the pipeline from end to end meant that they lost the most valuable contracts to the players that could. Together with the advent of wide-bodied aircraft with the capacity to carry large volumes of cargo with a full passenger load, yield decline became a common problem for the airline cargo management. The Cargo 2000 initiative grew out of the perceived need of the airlines to compete with the integrators and the objective of rapid, quality data exchange has now been brought under the e-freight banner.

4. Security

Undoubtedly the reason for most change and in particular the rapid increase in take-up of e-freight has been the new requirements relating to security; in fact the rate of change is about to increase. Since the atrocities of 9/11, authorities worldwide have become more attuned to the risks imposed by shipping freight by air. Interestingly it was not the Pan Am flight or the Indian Airlines flight – both brought down by bombs on board – that triggered the new requirements.

Until the security requirements were implemented, the consolidation manifest only existed in paper form on board the aircraft in the agent's pouch. The airline was prohibited from looking at the data as it was considered to be commercially sensitive. All that went by the board when the United States, closely followed by Canada and the EU, introduced regulations stating that shipment data at both master and house waybill level must be registered at the first airport of entry into a country five hours before arrival for a long-haul flight and on wheels-up for a short-haul flight. Domestic flights, for some reason, were exempt. The airline was made responsible for this data and fines would be imposed for late submission and errors, the latter reason being regarded by many as being short-sighted and possibly removing vital clues as to the 'secure status' of a shipment.

Suddenly airlines and handling agents worldwide had to receive, store and transmit not just the e-AWB but also house waybill data during the export process. Fines could be largely avoided by blanking out the optional data elements as no fines were imposed if they were blank – just if they were wrong.

Many IT companies saw an opportunity to build systems that took the data from several sources and amalgamated it into the format required by the US AMS system, Canada's ACI (Advanced Commercial Information) system or the EU's ICS (Import Control System). Descartes, SITA (CHAMP), ABS and many others created solutions without which a large number of airlines and GHAs could not have managed.

If the airlines had to capture this data manually, the load placed on the operation would have been extensive, with delays to shipments occurring with increased frequency. Nearly all the airlines started or re-energized existing e-AWB projects as a consequence. IATA is now reaping the benefits to its e-freight programme from these requirements.

Does it stop there? No, because as quickly as new security requirements are introduced, terrorist organizations find gaps or other methods of breaching the defences. Hence the reaction to the plot to blow up a plane where the explosive was found in the toner pack of a printer at an aircraft at East Midlands Airport, in England, in 2010.

The initial US reaction was to go for 100 per cent screening of inbound cargo but this was relaxed in favour of a combination of programmes that included screening, intelligence and focused bans. These are now in place but the stage is set for the next major upheaval in ACAS (Air Cargo Advanced Screening) or the EU's PRECISE (Pre-Departure/loading Consignment Information for Secure Entry). Canada is in on the game also with PACT (Pre-load Air Cargo Targeting). These schemes aim to identify illegal or undesirable cargo and prevent its loading onto the aircraft at the departure airport. Data has to be lodged five hours prior to departure, making it difficult for the airlines to comply as many shipments don't turn up until a few hours before departure. It may also have the impact of pushing the responsibility for data down to the forwarder and, therefore, give the for-warders the rationale for adopting e-freight as the airlines could legitimately offer different service levels for electronic shipments versus paper ones due to the security 'overhead'.

The role of the General Handling Agent

It is only recently that IATA and other organizations realized that they had to involve GHAs in discussions about e-freight and security programmes as airlines moved further and further away from operating their own physical cargo warehouses (sheds). In the 1960s major international airlines had a network of such facilities, but gradually in the 1990s these were subcontracted out as the yield decline started to bite and airlines fought to save money during the impact of the Gulf War and recession. Today the industry is dominated by a few very large global players such as Dnata, Swissport, Worldwide Freight Services (WFS), Cargo Airport Services (CAS USA) and Menzies World Cargo. Rationalization is increasing, with Swissport buying the Spanish company Flightcare and the French-owned Servisair in 2014. The e-freight and security programmes are impacting on the operations of the GHAs as airlines force them to meet the requirement as well as pressing them to reduce costs. Many airlines do not have their own cargo department at all, relying on the combination of a sales agent and a network of GHAs to perform the movement of freight and adherence to the relevant regulations. This makes the role of the GHA an increasingly important one.

The logistics pipeline for air freight carried on an airline can be shown as:

Shipper – Forwarder – GHA – Airline – GHA – Broker – Consignee

In reality it can be much more complicated. There may be a consolidator involved in exporting the goods (a means of benefiting from lower rates relating to a heavier shipment to the same destination), the airline portion may involve several flights and the importer may be a broker acting on behalf of several agents each dealing with their own part of the consolidated shipment.

In many respects dealing with freight is more complex than dealing with a passenger. The ticket is an airline-only (or its agent) document and e-tickets are now common. The air waybill is an international document in 11 parts that many Customs authorities require. Normally a passenger can find his or her own way to the gate but a box needs locating and moving and then there's the problem of locating freight and finding it again. You would be surprised how many UTLs exist (that's Unable To Locate).

I remember spending 45 minutes in the BA shed at LHR looking for a bright red Ferrari. Now you'd think that finding a bright red Ferrari would be easy, wouldn't you ? We found it eventually, but it wasn't red and didn't look like a Ferrari. That's because the car was in a box! A big box, mind you, but we were not looking for a box. This is just one example of how you cannot rely on the description on the waybill.

If the freight is a large shipment, it is quite possible that an airline will split it over several flights and, in the worst case, even airports, so that a part may go on one flight to JFK and another to Newark with a trucking leg involved to reunite them. Some Customs authorities do not allow split shipments to be cleared: you must have the whole shipment or you may have to clear and pay all the duties involved on the first part to arrive. These kinds of rules vary by country and sometimes by airport (as in Germany) or state (as in the United States). The pipeline roles (according to IATA) are shown in Figure 5.2.

1. Shipper

- Provides the cargo agent with hard copies of the shipping instruction and possibly scanned images or electronic versions of the trade documents, eg invoice, packing list and where legally feasible the Certificate of Origin.
- In some cases provides the consignee and the Customs broker/agent with electronic versions of the trade documents, eg invoice, packing list and where legally feasible the Certificate of Origin. Customs broker/agent and consignee may also be provided with electronic access to the trade documents, eg FTP or online using a third-party provider.
- Provides the consignee with hard copies of other documents legally required in paper format at destination via courier or by sending with the shipment.
- Submits the Customs export goods declaration to clear the goods for export.
- Ensures compliance with any dangerous goods packing and rules.

2. Cargo agent

- Creates and submits the air waybill as instructed by the shipper including the shipper's name in the air waybill (FWB) message information and arranges the booking.
- Places the air waybill, invoice, packing list, Certificate of Origin and freight invoice in the 'consolidation pouch' that travels with the shipment.
- Provides the shipper with the air waybill, which may be a scanned PDF copy or a signed paper copy of the original.

3. Carrier (self-handling example, could be subcontracted to a GHA)

- Receives the shipment with the 'pouch' from the cargo agent, makes it available at destination airport and notifies the Customs broker/agent/consignee.

FIGURE 5.2 Pipeline roles

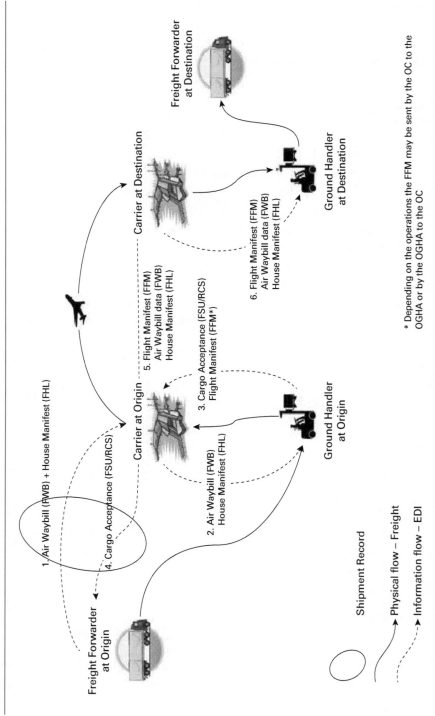

Freight Forwarder at Origin

1. Air Waybill (FWB) + House Manifest (FHL)

4. Cargo Acceptance (FSU/RCS)

Carrier at Origin

Carrier at Destination

Freight Forwarder at Destination

2. Air Waybill (FWB) House Manifest (FHL)

3. Cargo Acceptance (FSU/RCS) Flight Manifest (FFM*)

5. Flight Manifest (FFM) Air Waybill data (FWB) House Manifest (FHL)

6. Flight Manifest (FFM) Air Waybill data (FWB) House Manifest (FHL)

Ground Handler at Origin

Ground Handler at Destination

Shipment Record

Physical flow – Freight

Information flow – EDI

* Depending on the operations the FFM may be sent by the OC to the OGHA or by the OGHA to the OC

- Provides, if need be, a warehouse receipt to the cargo agent to confirm the freight weight, volume and number of pieces received.

- Lodges the Customs export cargo declaration at origin and the Customs import cargo declaration at destination to clear the cargo, providing any additional paper documents if requested.

- Delivers to destination airport and notifies the Customs broker/agent/consignee.

- Provides, if need be, a delivery note to the consignee at destination to confirm the freight weight, volume and number of pieces delivered.

4. Consignee

- Provides the Customs broker/agent with the paper or scanned invoice, packing list, and where legally feasible the Certificate of Origin as well as with hard copies of other documents via courier/post/hand prior to reception of the shipment.

- Receives arrival notification from the carrier at destination, when no 'Notify Party' is shown in the air waybill.

- Arranges pick-up and delivery of the shipment.

5. Customs broker/agent

- Receives from the consignee other paper documents that are legally required in paper format, eg CITES certificates, via courier directly.

- Receives from the carrier at destination or the GHA the arrival notification, as well as the air waybill together with the trade documents, eg invoice, packing list and where legally feasible the Certificate of Origin from the 'pouch' by courier.

- Prepares the Customs import goods declaration prior to the receipt of the shipment by the consignee.

- Lodges the Customs import goods declaration to clear the shipment providing any additional paper documents if requested.

- Undertakes ancillary services as instructed by the consignee, such as pick-up and delivery of the shipment.

6. GHA

Where the airline does not operate its own warehouse facility, a GHA may be used to provide those services at the departure point, destination, transit point, or all three. The GHA has to deal with all the Customs procedures relating to the handling of the goods:

- Receives the shipment with the 'pouch' from the cargo agent, and gives it to the ramp handling agent for transfer to the aircraft.

- Provides a warehouse receipt to the cargo agent to confirm the freight weight, volume and number of pieces received.

- Lodges the Customs export cargo declaration at origin and relays the data back to the carrier for onward transmission to destination.

- Imports: accepts the freight off the inbound flight and notifies the Customs broker/agent/consignee and provides, if need be, a delivery note to the receiving import broker/agent at destination to confirm the freight weight, volume and number of pieces delivered.

GHAs' IT history

At first, GHAs used the airlines' computer systems to run their sheds; this practice is still very prevalent especially in the United States where airlines have a strong influence and the home airlines' cargo systems tend to be very weak in terms of EDI. One major exception to this is Cargo Airport Services (CAS), which developed Ipic; it has used this to become the largest GHA in the Americas. For some reason, US airlines have not adopted EDI to the same extent as European or Eastern carriers and this is now holding them back with regards to modern requirements such as e-freight and security.

Very few GHAs created their own systems, even though using an airline's system did nothing for their business. How could you meet local Customs regulations or even charge for your services if the data resided in the airline system? In the United States it didn't matter too much. This is because the tendency there was for one airline to be housed in one warehouse, so if a GHA had three airlines contracted to it, it would have three separate facilities. Paper was used to control the business and this is still true today in the majority of US facilities.

Certain GHAs were not content with a paper-based system, so Cargo Service Centre (an off-shoot of KLM, now part of CAS) created its own system, CASCADE. In the United Kingdom ABS was already in the majority of facilities due to the UK Customs requirements for electronic inventory control, and a few GHAs in Scandinavia adopted the SITA FAST 4 system for their own use.

Lufthansa systems followed with its ELWIS system, which was installed all over Germany, and the massive Cargolux facility in Luxembourg. In the UK, with its special requirements, Lufthansa worked with BT to create its own GHA system COMET. The fact that this system looked very similar to ABS is probably down to the fact that BT also developed that system, thereby having two teams creating competing systems in the same technology at the same time in the same offices.

Nearly all these systems were created in the early 1990s with 'green screens' or if lucky DOS PCs. Technology was moving at a rapid pace, and two companies decided that the time was right for a new system. The British Airways software house Speedwing Logica created the Mercury handling system based on Oracle RDBMS and developed in the COOLGEN rapid development system. It had several successes in Indonesia, Kenya, Zimbabwe and Tanzania and captured a major customer in Ogden cargo. This system has been re-engineered and is now part of the GALAXY suite offered by Kale Consultants of India.

The second solution came from an established software company based in Switzerland. Software AG had created a modern PC-based GSA system called Cargo One and enhanced it to cover GHA functions. This was just a stepping stone to creating a full airline system known as CARGOSPOT, owned and marketed by CHAMP (a joint venture between Cargolux airlines and SITA).

In the early 2000s Menzies Cargo decided that it could create competitive advantage by developing its own system. It worked with external software houses, eventually forming a partnership with Magic software of Israel to create the HERMES system. This system had hand-held terminals and service-level management at the heart of its system and was a major leap forward in GHA operational systems. Needless to say, it took a long time for the other systems to catch up, but they have. Now, Hermes is not selling as well, support is an issue and the big screens showing service levels have vanished from the Heathrow sheds.

Today, the market is dominated by a few solutions. ELWIS is still there in about 18 sites but signs of its replacement are appearing, such as a recent RFP issued to replace it at a major German airport. I am not aware of any new major sale of this system for several years and LIS seems to have stopped or curtailed its marketing of this product.

Cargospot is the dominant system outside the UK. In particular it is the standard solution employed by the two largest GHAs in the world: WFS and Swissport. It is, however, suffering from the number of installations (as each country has its own idiosyncrasies) and age and is likely to be replaced within a few years.

Kale is marketing the GALAXY system and has picked up Bahrain as its latest customer plus others in India. ABS has just released its ABS5 system, which includes the latest warehouse management system and truck handling and is one of the major players with over 100 sites utilizing its product. It has already replaced HERMES within one major Spanish organization and is likely to do the same for others in Europe. The key to its resurgence is the level of investment in the product each year together with the support given to all customers so that even its newest customers can utilize the system to its full extent. The GHA sector is one where the IT systems need continuous investment to remain legal as well as competitive, but with the airlines only bothered about reducing costs, how can the GHA afford to continue to fund the changes required?

Conclusions

The air freight business as regards airlines is still tens of years behind the passenger business in adopting e-trade standards and procedures. There are many reasons for this that are heavily entrenched in the parties involved. The IATA e-freight programme is running way behind schedule and will continue to do so as long as the airlines keep using antiquated systems and demand GHAs use them instead of generic GHA programmes. Airlines do not realize that if the GHA has no system of its own, without a paper trail it cannot accept e-freight consignments. While IATA has tried to identify the procedures involved in e-freight, it ignores many aspects such as the forwarder delivery and pick-up process and all the processes that take place in the warehouse. E-freight is not going to become the normal method of doing business unless all parties in the supply chain adopt it and back it with system changes.

The new security initiatives requiring data five hours before departure are likely to have a major positive impact on the availability of data from shippers and forwarders, and this will put the responsibility for data quality where it belongs – at the start of the supply chain. The airlines will benefit from this availability of electronic data, but only those that re-engineer their processes to eliminate paper within their own businesses will reap the financial rewards. The next few years are going to be very interesting as finally the air freight business is forced to change. In the GHA business, rationalization seems to be the order of the day but this can only go so far until competition is reduced and new operators see an opportunity. GHA contracts tend to be very short-lived with get-out clauses of one to three months common. Customer churn is a fact of life for GHAs but the continual reduction in price will have to stop at some point otherwise there will be a major corporate failure that will have far-reaching consequences for this business. Airlines need to focus on quality of handling, adherence to regulations and exchange of accurate data to move this business forward.

Road feeder service

06

On the road

Air cargo spends only 10 to 20 per cent of its journey time in the air, the remainder on the ground. Time on the ground is taken up with ground handling, which in most cases also involves road transport of some kind. If road feeder service (RFS) for air cargo connectivity, especially between airports, is therefore considered as an integral part of ground handling, it can be identified as the least controllable link in the chain. The road transport element between shipper, through the air freight process and finally to the customer, is one of the most critical, expensive and delay-prone components of air logistics, carrying goods to and from airports as well as, in some cases, delivering direct to customers. Each world region operates a different method, style and level of efficiency in providing RFS, depending on the local conditions and regulations, quality of roads and geographical area covered.

For example, Cargolux Airlines, based in Luxembourg, has built its highly successful long-haul freight business by bringing all its cargo by road to its base and operating a fleet of B747 freighters to its many worldwide destinations. The same process is applied in reverse to import goods. The company works with some 20 different trucking companies, serving over 40 airports, resulting in around 47,000 truck movements each year. It is, however, atrociously expensive, some estimates up to €100 million per year, and is therefore constantly under scrutiny and revision.

The United States, the biggest market in the world, has developed a fast nationwide interstate highway system consisting of around 77,000 kms, which links the entire country in a fast and efficient way. This means that most goods are transported internally over vast distances by truck, which is cheaper by far than flying, reliable and efficient. Average running speeds of around 121 kmh are normal, depending on different state regulations. Goods for export or import are thus delivered and collected for international flight connections at major hubs, very often with specialized roller bed trucks, configured to handle up to four and sometimes five pre-built aircraft Unit Load Devices (ULD). Transportation between airports is therefore at least daily, and in some cases hourly in frequency.

The integrators are thus handling the most urgent and express traffic for internal customers, first for efficiency and cost, but also as a strategic tool especially in case of inclement weather. Miami Airport is an interesting example of passenger and cargo traffic functioning in parallel. Known informally as the capital of Latin America, Miami's airport is one of the busiest cargo hubs in the United States, especially for perishable goods. The flow of goods from South and Central America is largely channelled through Miami, including flowers, fruit and vegetables. Thanks to a comprehensive route network, goods that are not destined for the United States are transited to other worldwide destinations. A road corridor links the airport cargo area to the warehouse zone and thence to the interstate highway system. Around 200,000 separate truck movements are executed annually. Similarly Los Angeles (LAX) handles some 2 million tons of cargo each year, most of which is through Far East trade, primarily with Japan, China and South Korea.

In India, a series of high-quality highways is under construction but there is much ground to make up to satisfy the needs of manufacturing companies. Fewer than 5 million kms of modern and unpaved roads serve the country but it was only after 1995 that the programme really started. By 2013, some 21 thousand kms of four- to six-lane highways had been brought into use. The poor quality of many unpaved rural roads has made it difficult for farmers trying to transport their produce to distribution points, and perishables remain a key air export commodity. There is still a large proportion of rigid trucks with two or three axles capable of carrying between 9 and 25 tons, whereas the European five-axle articulated trucks could carry 40 tons. DHL says that the 2,000 km run between New Delhi and Bangalore or Mumbai to Delhi takes around 35 hours while the same distance in Europe would average 11 to 12 hours and in China 17 to 18 hours. India has 20 international airports but most cargo moves through Delhi and Mumbai. Road transport inefficiency has had some benefits for airlines operating freighters, however, as direct services to key regional hubs or even direct to Europe can still demand premium pricing as the clients have little option to use alternate gateways.

The European market

To illustrate the complexities of RFS, we have taken a detailed look at the European market and included comments from some of the companies selected.

Paul Bodde, Managing Director of GSSA Kales Germany GmbH, is full of praise:

> Due to their reliability both Sovereign Speed and haulier BTW Transporte have become our preferred partners for feeding shipments from Central Europe to Heathrow where some of our mandate airlines like Virgin Atlantic or Air New Zealand operate.

What Paul does not mention is that without these trucking services he could hardly forward any air freight from continental Europe to the UK. Hence, he'd be out of business. Air New Zealand together with Kales's other mandate airlines operating to and from London would have a much smaller volume of cargo. Consequently, this would have a tremendous negative impact. Likewise, European airlines operating in the UK, mostly with narrow-body aircraft, would have a hard time offering a competitive product without efficient RFS between UK gateways and Europe.

Trucking has become an indispensable part of the supply chain for getting boxes and packages from the shipper's facility to the airport, or in the opposite direction in case of imports. But the vast majority of air cargo in Europe travels on specialized tractor trailer units, specifically tasked for the efficient movement of complete ULDs, allowing a minimization of costs, almost entirely eliminating damage, and also ensuring in the case of perishables a temperature-controlled environment. Most road feeder services crossing Europe operated or controlled by airlines run under an airlines flight number; AF/KLM, BA and Lufthansa Cargo's trucks are excellent examples.

How vital trucking services are for keeping the global economy running and supplying retailers with goods was illustrated when the Icelandic volcano Eyjafjallajoekull erupted in March 2010, bringing air traffic in most parts of Europe to a complete standstill. 'Unable to air freight our goods, we trucked our shipments from Germany and other countries of origin during those days to Istanbul where the ash cloud hadn't reached,' said a DHL spokesman.

Similarly in Iceland, local carrier Icelandair had to relocate all flights from Keflavik airport near Reykjavik to Akureyri in the far north of the island, where the local skies were not affected by the volcanic cloud due to favourable drifts. 'Particularly many of our fish consignments bound to

Canada and the USA had to be trucked all the way up north to Akureyri to circumvent the ash cloud and have them flown out,' recalls Gunnar Sigurffinsson, Icelandair's Head of Cargo. This highlights the fact that, as in the United States, the integrators ensuring an efficient ground network reinforce air capabilities, trucking always will retain its close link to air cargo as a key component, or for its flexibility to meet emergency circumstances.

Road feeding as business saver

In most parts of Europe, there are many different types of road feeder services. They differ in products, service, networks and reliability. Problems can occur when failures in communication interrupt traffic flows. For example, a recent incident occurred when a shipment dispatched by a shipper located in Germany booked on a certain flight bound for China was eagerly expected to arrive by road. Since time was running out the local handling agent called the shipper asking for the whereabouts of the goods and was told that the truck was still parked near the warehouse in which the shipment was stored. The Slovenian drivers, not speaking any German or English, sat in their cab waiting for some warehouse personnel to inform them when the loading of the items could begin. The Frankfurt handling agent was informed but the shipment missed its flight. This is an example of the pitfalls that can occur when seeking the lowest price, usually offered by trucking companies that would otherwise return home empty, instead charging rock-bottom prices if the destination is on route.

A better and more promising solution is to rely on trucking firms that might charge a bit more but are specialized in air cargo and deliver good and constant quality and communicate proactively. 'When choosing our trucking partners we always ranked the quality aspect first. This fundamental decision paid off up to now and is also welcomed by most clients when thoroughly explained to them,' states Kales Manager Paul Bodde. On average, the GSSA fills 10 trucks each week with goods to be transported from Germany to Heathrow. 'However, there are some weeks the number of trucks we need to carry our air freight exports to the UK goes up to 20,' he says.

The specialized RFS carriers have invested in training, sophisticated IT solutions, GPS tracking, safety and security and reliability. Sometimes the expression 'penny wise and pound foolish' is very applicable in this business.

In contrast to BTW that accepts only full truckload assignments, Hamburg-headquartered Sovereign Speed takes any order from clients, irrespective of size or weight. This less than trailer load (LTL) business model is highly attractive for many forwarders or handling agents, because it assures them utmost flexibility at all times. Shipments collected late afternoon or early evening all over Central Europe are consolidated around midnight at Cologne or Frankfurt and then handed to the airlines or their agents at London Heathrow or Paris CDG early next morning. This service has become extremely attractive for many industrial players as it bypasses night flight bans in hubs such as Frankfurt, since the only option to get air freight overnight from Rhine-Main airport to Amsterdam, Vienna or London is by using hauliers.

Founded in 1998, Sovereign Speed is still a fairly young enterprise that keeps spreading its wings. Meanwhile, the service firm's sprinter fleet and trucks are a common sight on autobahns and highways, especially at night when Sovereign's transport is at its peak. 'We figured out that there is sufficient demand for fast and reliable transport of express shipments throughout Europe each night and that surface haulage would be the most suitable, flexible and also promising solution to offer the market,' says El-Sayegh. As of today, his firm operates a fleet of more than 120 GPS-equipped vehicles, predominantly trucks but also 30 sprinters.

The company's main routes are those that link Europe's major cargo gateways – Frankfurt, Paris CDG, Brussels, Heathrow or Amsterdam, acting as a cargo airline on wheels, ensuring extremely fast transport solutions for shipments from one kilogram to large loads, as well as fixed departure and arrival times. All transport routes are carried out according to a fixed schedule. They are operated six nights per week to over 55 destinations all across Central and Western Europe. At each major gateway Sovereign has established its own offices, for instance in AMS, LHR, CDG, BRU, CGN, FRA and MUC, to ensure proper handling and operations according to customers' demands. Sovereign's business strategy is based on three pillars:

1 The constant increase of the average load factor on all existing routes, to steadily increase the firm's profitability.

2 Integrating at least two new stations each consecutive year to the network, to increase local commercial activities, widen the reach, and gain additional market knowledge.

3 Adding new products to the existing portfolio, such as different door-to-door services, Customs clearance of shipments, transport of dangerous goods or X-ray security controls.

The company operates as a neutral and independent cargo carrier collaborating only with forwarding agents, integrators, GSAs and cargo airlines.

A somewhat different business model providing everything from a single source and built on modular solutions is offered by Dutch transporting giant Jan de Rijk Logistics. The company stands for those kind of market players that provide abundant capacity, offer their clients pan-European scheduled services and have representation or own offices at most major airports within the EU. Addressing a broad range of sectors, market leader Jan de Rijk has built up particular expertise in key industries such as air freight, automotive, aerospace, high-tech and electronics, retail, healthcare and perishables.

In addition to RFS, the Roosendaal-headquartered firm engages increasingly in rail transport and warehousing, thus offering clients a comprehensive service portfolio. Most of the company's own vehicles are equipped with on-board computers, enabling real-time data transmission and hence the option to directly manage the fleet. This communication tool helps to improve operational efficiency as well as customer service.

Basically, all major airlines serving Europe are in business relations in one way or another with the Dutch haulier. This is the result of the company's excellent reputation for quality and efficiency combined with a dense road feeder network that covers the entire continent.

According to CEO Sebastiaan Scholte his firm currently deploys 850 vehicles, of which 35 per cent belong to subcontractors. These partners 'we screen thoroughly to make sure they keep up to our own standards, including security training of their drivers'. Due to cost reasons about 50 per cent of Jan de Rijk's fleet is operating with a licence from one of the Eastern European countries. Price pressure is enormous but again, if customers opt for product quality, they are not well advised to choose the cheapest market player for performing their road transport. Cheap can become expensive very quickly if mistakes happen or drivers are not able to understand the contents of declarations on dangerous goods or other documents accompanying shipments.

Air freight accounts for 40 per cent of the Dutch company's business, with 60 per cent related to warehousing, rail transport and other segments. 'In case of a crisis it's better to have more than one egg in the basket,' Sebastiaan states. He speaks of 'three drivers for profitability', all of which must be met to end up in the black:

1 high load factors throughout the year;

2 sufficient yields per kilogram and driven kilometres; and

3 constant utilization of the rolling asset.

Scholte says:

> Considering the predatory competition we need to drive as many kilometres as possible to balance our fixed costs. However, bottlenecks and slow throughput of shipments at major airports are increasingly hindering trucking firms from running their vehicles on schedule. The results are supply chain disruptions and reduced quality of air freight processes. What we and other road feeder service providers urgently need are fast turn-around times at gateways, thus enabling a seamless flow of shipments and a constant usage rate of our vehicles.

Lately, things have taken a turn for the worse, with waiting times getting longer and longer, particularly at large hubs like Amsterdam, Frankfurt, Heathrow or Charles de Gaulle. The downtime for his and other firms is growing constantly, especially at peak times each Friday and Monday. He blames the low margins in air freight handling for the mess. Why, the manager also indicates:

> Because labour is the biggest cost factor for handlers, they don't increase their staff on days with heavy traffic in order to prevent additional expenditures in personnel. Even if they would like to hire more staff their capabilities are very limited due to the extremely low margins obtainable in this fiercely competitive field. Therefore, slower air freight processing within the handling agent's warehouses is the obvious consequence. The entire case wouldn't be as harmful for trucking firms if the handlers would communicate any congestion or delayed pick-up times at an early stage, which most of them unfortunately do not. In that case we would be able to reroute our trucks and change their schedules at short notice.

Given this, it seems obvious that if we are to improve the transit times for scheduled air cargo and make it competitive again, this is one area that TIACA and IATA should be focusing on. The RFS trucking companies are crying out for efficiency improvements that could only benefit everyone in the supply chain.

Meanwhile, another major RFS supplier Wallenborn is in the starting blocks to take the next step: expanding into growing markets outside the EU. He speaks of the United States, Latin America and the Middle East being under close consideration. Says the manager: 'Currently we are talking to potential partners, but nothing has been concluded at this stage.' Wallenborn has even expressed interest in opening in China, no doubt to serve Cargolux and AirBridgeCargo, two of its biggest European clients.

So what about the hundreds of small and medium-sized players that are trucking goods from airport to airport and try to stay in business? Almost all of them lack the capacity and financial resources to challenge the big operators like Jan de Rijk, Arthur Welter, Wallenborn, DB Schenker, Panalpina and others. They basically have three choices to survive:

1 the independent: deciding on standing alone as long as possible operating as a niche player;
2 becoming a subcontractor of one of the larger enterprises;
3 joining forces and forming their own alliances.

Living example: RunAir

The alliance concept has been practised since 2012 by eight individual trucking firms located at different cities and regions all over Germany. Facing the predatory market conditions they opted for offering their clients similar services at identical prices, for instance, charges for X-raying and security controls of goods, storing and repacking of items, labelling and documentation of shipments. Their deal includes a guarantee to refrain from approaching any potential customer based in a region that belongs to the home territory of another neighbouring RunAir affiliate. All members offer road feeder transport of air freight from their individual sites to Rhine-Main Airport, where the local RunAir staff consolidates the shipments that are to be flown out of the country. Goods that are for domestic customers are handed over to the responsible RunAir partner for onward transportation within Germany. This results in trade lanes leading from Hamburg via Frankfurt to Munich or Dusseldorf–Frankfurt–Stuttgart, just to illustrate two examples of fast and efficient overnight transport by truck via the group's consolidation centre at Frankfurt Airport. By doing so, they basically are following the hub model of the integrators, with the sole difference that the RunAir consignments are not flown but transported overnight by truck or van.

Similar to Sovereign Speed the trucking alliance also accepts LTL orders. This could be a single piece that needs to be transported or go up to shipments weighing five tons or more.

Lately, the eight group members have taken the initiative to extend their pact by collaborating with other European trucking companies. One such candidate that had successfully been approached is Madrid-based company Ibertinsa. At an initial joint meeting held in Hamburg in 2013, Ibertinsa's Managing Director Manuel Corominas's first words were that he can't bear hearing the word 'crisis' any longer: 'Instead, I rather prefer talking about the many opportunities our individual home markets are currently offering.' According to Señor Corominas, due to the country's exceptionally high unemployment rate, which led to a sharp drop in private consumption, Spain has been badly hit by massive import problems. There is simply a lack of buying power, hurting the entire economy, he stated. However, the manager also mentioned a light at the end of the dark tunnel: 'Spanish exports are running very well, up 14 per cent in average year-on-year.'

So despite the current crisis in Spain, Portugal and most of southern Europe, there is still a substantial market demand for transporting goods across the old continent, he concluded. This could ensure the basic capacity utilization of trucking services on the North–South corridor. In addition, this initial tonnage could be supplemented by intercontinental air freight shipments. This was the basic and simple idea behind the strategic pact formed between the RunAir Group and Ibertinsa. Indeed, many shipments arriving in Frankfurt on board Lufthansa Cargo's fleet, AirBridgeCargo's, Cathay Pacific's freighter aircraft or those of other carriers serving Rhine-Main, Madrid or Barcelona are transit cargoes that need onward transportation to get to their final consignees.

According to Ibertinsa's Manuel Corominas and his RunAir counterparts Sven Zelmer and Detlef Warburg, there is a huge opportunity to tap a great portion of this road feeder volume running from Germany to Spain and vice versa by collaborating closely. 'We have the trucks and the drivers, the tonnage is there, so let's go,' Corominas concluded. How this is functioning practically is demonstrated by Amsterdam-based forwarding agent Interport BV that partnered some time ago with Ibertinsa by forming a joint venture. 'We managed to become the market leader in air freight trucking between the Netherlands, Spain and Portugal,' reported Interport's MD Wilma Bram at the Hamburg gathering. She had more impressive figures to present: 'Our claim ratio is 0.02 per cent on average and 99.2 per cent of the entire loads are delivered on time to their customers,' Wilma said.

Something similar will now be set up between the RunAir Group and Ibertinsa on trucking routes between Germany and Spain, although not as joint venture but on pure marketing conditions. Operationally this means that the eight members comprising the RunAir Group will feed all shipments originating from Germany and going to Spain into Frankfurt for consolidation. This includes line-haul trucking services from places like Cologne, Hamburg, Stuttgart, Munich and other major German cities to Rhine-Main. Once in Frankfurt these domestically produced goods will be bundled to new loads by combining them with the intercontinental volumes arriving by air and destined for the Iberian Peninsula. 'Through this move we extend our mainly domestic network considerably by tapping into the Spanish market,' stated RunAir's MD Detlef Warburg.

The necessary infrastructure is in place with Ibertinsa providing trucks and drivers. RunAir's task is to manage the entire road feeder service between Germany and Spain through the group's Frankfurt office. As agreed between the two parties these scheduled trucking services linking Rhine-Main with Barcelona's and Madrid's airports are three times a week, on Monday, Wednesday and Friday. 'We guarantee a driving time of 48 hours each way between the three gateways. For beyond shipments going to Seville, Valencia or other Spanish cities we need an additional 24 hours,' said Ibertinsa's MD Corominas. He announced integrating Portugal in the pan-European line-haul service after the Spain runs have been established. Strategic plans for expanding the operational network are a rather small but promising step in Ibertinsa's and RunAir's mutual fight against the ongoing economic crisis in most parts of southern Europe and their joint effort to stay in the highly competitive market of European RFS.

Conclusions

Although there has been much discussion over the last 30 years on substituting rail transport for road feeder, the truck remains the most flexible and cost-effective way of linking airports with customers. However, a rail connection between China and Europe has been successfully started and others may well follow in the future. We have seen how the trucking sector is calling out for change, and it is our conclusion that only through effective communication and joint efforts can trucking companies, ground handlers and airports become once again efficient and effective tools for the airlines in improving capability to compete. Days not hours can be saved in the logistics supply chain if this could happen. The examples from Europe may not apply to other regions of the world, due to local roads, regulations, traffic flows and the distances involved. All countries, however, share the same basic need to take export goods to the airport or sea port and to collect and distribute imports. In the global market, efficient road transport becomes increasingly important as logistics companies are forced to deliver goods faster and without mistakes.

Freight forwarder

07

The role of the freight forwarder or forwarding agent has today evolved to become a multifaceted operator acting between the shipper and customer, taking responsibility for shipments to the handling agent and the eventual delivery of the shipments quickly and in good condition to the destination or consignee. The forwarder will take responsibility for the goods, ensure that they conform to the international regulations for the transportation of goods by air, including dangerous goods regulations and documentation, and pass them to a cargo ground handler at the airport of departure.

At the destination airport, the corresponding forwarder, either a branch of the same company or another designated agent, will deliver the shipment to its final customer. A forwarder should be an expert in supply chain management and have good contacts with airlines or charter brokers to negotiate the best price or conditions for transport.

The forwarder prepares and processes the documentation including Customs and export declarations, dangerous goods, air waybills and the other required documentation. In some cases there may be as many as 30 paper documents prepared for a single air freight shipment. To improve this process, which takes time and is becoming increasingly expensive, considerable efforts are being made by the controlling bodies such as TIACA and IATA to gain acceptance of paperless electronic processing. There has been much resistance to this initiative by the forwarders, which they often perceive as a highly expensive process compared to the yields.

In some countries freight agents may also act as Customs brokers and need the relevant government licence. In the case of the very large forwarders, or logistics services providers, registration and licensing with the national government may be mandatory.

The development of the forwarder

The work carried out by forwarders has become more detailed and sophisticated over the last two decades. Although there are many small to medium-sized companies in nearly every country, the business is dominated by the top 25 that operate in the multimodal global market. In some cases the very large multinational freight forwarders may operate their own flights in order to consolidate freight accumulated from various clients. The leading multimodal IATA forwarders include: DHL with Exel USA, Kuehne & Nagel, DB Schenker, Panalpina, UPS, Sinotrans, Ceva Logistics, Expeditors, SDV + Bollore, DSV, Nippon Express, Damco, CH Robinson, KWE, Toll, Glovis, Kintetsu, Agility Logistics, Hellmann Worldwide, Logwin, Geodis and Yusen.

Freight forwarders receive payment from their customers. With the addition of fuel surcharges and other special costs these transactions may involve complex calculations. By using an electronic processing system, forwarders are able to prepare cargo manifests in advance, a legal necessity in many countries; they can also track the shipments – or enable their clients to do so – and calculate invoices.

The cargo accounts settlement system (CASS) is an IATA initiative, which provides a neutral settlement system between the airlines and the freight agents. This method of accounts settlement is now in operation in over 70 countries and offers protection for the carriers against unpaid invoices.

As many of the world's huge number of freight forwarders are independent, many organizations have grown up to support them, and in some cases represent their interests to government bodies such as the Customs authorities. In most countries there is at least one and sometimes several associations of freight agents that represent the interests of their national members. In addition, several private fee-paying groups assist their members in dealing with legislation and form working partnerships around the world. Some examples are: AICBA (Association of International Customs and Border Agencies) in Ottawa, Canada; CIFA, the Chinese International Freight Forwarders Association of Beijing China; HAFFA, the Hong Kong Association of Freight Forwarding & Logistics; JAFA, the Japan Air Freight Association, based in Tokyo, Japan; ACN, Air Cargo Netherlands in Amsterdam; NTC – the National Transport Committee, Riyadh, Saudi Arabia; SAAA, the Singapore Aircargo Agents Association; NAFL (National Association of Freight and Logistics) in Dubai; and the British International Freight Association (BIFA) in the UK.

FIATA (Fédération Internationale des Associations de Transitaires et Assimilés) – the International Federation of Air Freight Agents – was founded in 1926. This non-governmental organization currently represents around 40,000 multimodal forwarders and logistics companies employing some 10 million people in 150 countries. It cooperates closely with government and international authorities in the field of transport including IATA.

For independent freight agents there are various solutions for working with a network of other similar agents in other countries. Some private networks organized by the agents themselves function efficiently but great care is always needed in choosing a partner in another country due to the possibility of fraud or malpractice.

A number of networks have been set up with paid membership where the aim is to represent their members within the international market as a combined partnership able to compete with the global giants of the freight forwarding world. Examples of these are: EFFA – the European Freight Forwarders Association; the FFSI Global network in Hong Kong, which has members in 68 countries; GLA – Global Logistics Associates – of the Netherlands; the Security Cargo Network in Denver, USA; the Bangkok-headquartered WCA Family of Logistics Networks with over 4,000 members in 170 countries; Project Cargo Network (PCN) with members in 465 worldwide offices across 81 countries; and the Worldwide Project Consortium (WWPC) network.

Associations and networks

Due to the global nature of the air freight industry and indeed transportation in general, over 200 countries have their own national freight forwarder associations. Their task is to represent their members, organize conferences, training courses and represent them in international matters. Examples of these are: Airmail Panel (AMP), Cargo 2000, Cargo Agency Conference, Cargo Business Processes Panel (CBPP), Cargo Committee (CC), Cargo Data Interchange Task Force (CDITF), Cargo Operations Advisory Group, Cargo Procedures Conferences Management Group (CPCMG), Cargo Security Task Force, Cargo Services Conference (CSC), Cargo XML Task Force, Customs Advisory Group, Dangerous Goods Accredited Training School Network (ATS), Dangerous Goods Board (DGB), Dangerous Goods Training Task Force (DGTTF), e-AWB Advisory Group, Global Air Cargo Advisory Group, IATA Ground Operations Manual Task Force (IGOM), IATA/FIATA Consultative Council (IFCC), IATA/FIATA Customs Working Group, Interline Prorate Advisory Committee (IPAC), Live Animals and Perishables Board (LAPB), and Time and Temperature Task Force (TTTF).

OAG Cargo publishes data for forwarders including published real-time rates, route planning and operational data: **www.oag.com**. There is also the *A–Z Worldwide Airfreight Directory*; see **www.azfreight.com**.

CASE STUDY   Hellmann Worldwide

Matthew Marriott, former Commercial Director of Hellmann Worldwide Logistics UK

As one of the world's leading forwarders, this Europe-based company operates in a wide range of business sectors globally and is a typical example of the modern multimodal logistics provider.

To the uninitiated, the world of modern logistics is a dense, multifaceted and fiendishly complex industry; with ever advancing technology layering over reams of international legislation. But while technology and Customs wrangling are very much part of the modern industry, the basic principles of logistics, which must always be at the heart of everything, remain the same. Getting something from A to B within a certain time frame is the eternal mission – and while that might not always be the easiest requirement to meet, it is clear, simple and fundamental.

When you look at the logistics industry in its current incarnation with the modern pressures of road, sea and air freight, plus the scale and scope of the services available, it can easily seem as though it no longer bears any relation to that core purpose. But while it may well be unrecognizable in comparison to what it was 50 years ago, that is only the inevitable result of a period in history in which the whole landscape of commerce has altered without precedent. As such, it was inevitable that our industry would have to embrace these changes in order to remain competitive in the global environment. Of course, the world will always need products and materials to be transported to and from market, but if established providers were not able or willing to adapt to a changing climate, then they would have been quickly overtaken by those who could. Perhaps driven by that knowledge, logistics providers did change, and the industry has evolved its methodology and the management of its day-to-day operations in a transformative way.

Indeed, to put this into a personal context, within my 20-year career the demands of logistics have changed before my eyes. However, perhaps going back even further – to the origins of how Hellmann was first founded – provides an even clearer example of the evolutions of service that have occurred in the relatively recent past.

For Hellmann, it began in 1871 with Carl Heinrich Hellmann, who used a horse-drawn cart to deliver parcels in and around the town of Osnabruck in northern Germany. Well over a century later the only practical similarity is the family name, with Carl Heinrich's great grandchildren, Jost and Klaus, now owning and running the company across 157 countries globally. Quite a change, and symptomatic of just how far logistics has come. Of course, a natural part of Hellmann's modern service is air freight – a service that would have been utterly inconceivable back in 1871!

Air freight

Modern freight forwarding, and air freight, encompasses far more than it used to. These days a provider must be able to offer its customers much more than a rough shipment time frame; indeed a quick look at our own list of air freight services tells its own story. Hellmann currently offers:

- daily consolidation;
- IATA direct loading;
- strategic gateways;
- full and partial charters;
- on-board courier services;
- Customs brokerage;
- import, export and trans-shipments;
- handling of heavy and/or dangerous goods;
- assembly and distribution;
- packaging, crating, and short-term warehousing;
- palletized cargo; and
- global preferred carriers.

As you can see, it's as comprehensive as it is complex, and increasingly air freight providers are moving towards large-scale bespoke services for individual clients. However, the basic modern service will naturally include use of global data networks, monitoring direct flights, consolidations and both door-to-door and express traffic. It would also most likely incorporate warehouse networks, temporary storage and 'just-in-time' deliveries. Furthermore, the most successful carriers will have the resource and scope to be able to transport a huge variety of cargo types, from heavy loads to hazardous goods.

All of which, you will be unsurprised to know, is likely to be managed by huge global, state-of-the-art IT systems allowing real-time status information to be available along the entire supply chain; from initial pick-up to final delivery. Indeed, the availability of this technology represented true progress, with incredible implications for both the efficiency and customer service of operations in all areas of forwarding and logistics. In current times, of course, it's easy to forget the impact of IT, but, for forward-thinking providers such as ourselves, it really changed the game.

That said, despite the increasing mechanization and technology of logistics, there is still a huge need for the human element. A global industry requires a global understanding of Customs procedures; and that's no small matter. Negotiating Customs clearance is far from easy, and requires staff who are able to unpick tangled legislation – often in several languages. Obviously, this becomes even more important when EU-based companies are forwarding to countries outside the EU. One way around these challenges for both air and sea freight is to offer a brokerage service that makes use of local knowledge and expertise to smooth what can otherwise be a bumpy passage. For example, it is crucial to make sure all documentation is prepared prior to the shipment, so as to pre-empt any specific issues that might otherwise have to be resolved on arrival. Likewise, local offices at key destinations are really useful so that if problems do arise, there are people on the ground with the knowledge and experience to deal with them. This is an aspect of Hellmann's network that I personally think has played a really key role in our continued growth and development across the world.

People power

As I touched upon in the previous section, one of our industry's most pressing issues is one of recruitment. For all sorts of reasons, logistics, and particularly air freight, requires the human sensibility – the sort of wisdom and expertise that it's simply not possible to get from even the most technologically advanced IT system. Unfortunately, logistics as a global industry has a bit of an image problem; and in an age when more people leave education with academic degrees than not, the prospect of logistics is not necessarily going to be the biggest draw. As such, when asked what they want to do when they are older, children invariably aspire to professions that offer greater 'glamour', or the opportunity to be widely recognized in a variety of professional and personal contexts.

Unfortunately, in the unforgiving realities of the real world, and particularly in an economic climate that has squeezed employment opportunities, it is often the less publicized industries that really need the next generation of workplace talent. But regrettably, air logistics rarely incites the same level of enthusiasm in the minds of our young people as the idea of being, for example, an actor, footballer or pop star. Naturally, this can make it very hard for some industries to maintain growth and development.

This might be a slightly glib way to illustrate the point, but the underlying fact remains: there is a serious gap in young people's knowledge in regard to some of the UK's major industries, and particularly that of air freight. Indeed, this is even more of an issue when you consider that, despite perceptions, the wider logistics industry actually has a number of attributes that would almost certainly appeal to ambitious graduates; our industry simply needs to find a way to convey this message if it is to attract the top talent that it really needs.

However, before I, or indeed anyone else, can begin to extol the oft-concealed virtues of the work, there are some quite serious issues to conquer first. In 2012, PwC released a report that outlined a number of extremely worrying conclusions about the state of the global transportation and logistics industry. They were conclusions that made clear that it is not merely problems of perception that the industry should be concerned about. In comparison to other industries, salary levels are low, while training and development are insufficient in terms of providing the type of opportunities employees might look for. Indeed, the report found that there was only a 36 per cent probability that people will find the sector 'attractive' to work within by 2030. Translated into commercial terms, this means that the industry needs to undergo a substantial overhaul to stay competitive in the coming decades. Things may well have improved since 2012 in line with a general upturn in economic fortunes, but certainly not by enough to eradicate such concerns. It is sobering stuff.

And yet, in the words of Klaus-Dieter Ruske, PwC's global Transportation and Logistics Leader, despite the 'poor image, poor pay and poor prospects' that currently choke the industry, the reality is that there are 'rewarding, multinational opportunities out there that need tapping into'. Quite! These 'multinational opportunities' might well be one of the industry's greatest attributes in terms of drawing in talent.

Logistics and freight forwarding – and particularly air freight – by their very nature, are a truly global enterprise. Even for small companies that transport primarily within a particular country, they will most likely have to develop international relations, while bigger companies will have offices across the world. From the perspective of a young graduate, or indeed anyone looking to forge a career, this is often a hugely attractive prospect, providing a glimpse of opportunity and possibility that can be as aspirational as it is exciting.

But, while the industry absolutely does need those top graduates, it also needs people who are not necessarily academic, but who have the spark and drive to really rise up through companies. In my opinion, a company leader who has worked through all levels of an air freight business – from packing freight and loading an aircraft to making daily management decisions – is likely to be better equipped than one who has earned their stripes in university and theoretical management courses. Of course, this is not to say that university is not a superb provider of skills (Hellmann has run an extremely successful graduate scheme for the last six years), but simply that by framing your experience in practical knowledge, rather than solely theory, is an attribute than can be invaluable. It can give another dimension to management and leadership, with a whole resource of specific experience, understanding and even empathy for that individual to draw upon.

What this means is that air freight is an industry that has opportunities for a huge variety of skills – and not simply those dependent on a good degree from a red-brick. This should be a major strength of the industry, but in my opinion, not enough is being done by companies to communicate it. Put simply, there *needs* to be a commitment to *invest* in talent. There needs to be an assessment of recruiting processes, and perhaps even more importantly, the systems that they have in place in terms of developing employees.

Management schemes (open to all educational backgrounds) *and* graduate schemes cost money to implement, but not only do they offer the company the chance to develop the skills that its personnel require, they demonstrate the sort of commitment towards employee training and wellbeing that can really help fight against some of the superficial, yet powerful, negatives of external perception. Those who come through company schemes and go on to have dynamic careers within the sector will be walking exponents and advocates of the logistics profession. It is an incredibly effective method, and one that benefits the sector at every level.

This is certainly not an issue that the air freight and logistics industry faces in isolation, but neither does that diminish the importance of taking action now and turning attitudes around. Children might not have to say that they want to grow up to be a freight forwarder, but graduates and young professionals really do – and it is up to those within the industry to make sure that is the case.

Example: fashion

To give a fuller picture of how modern air freight works, I want to use one particular client as an example. The client is a United States-based global fashion retailer, and we have been working successfully with them for over three years.

The air freight service that we provide for this customer is a prime example of lean thinking; the notion that processes and methodologies are designed to create maximum efficiency right through the supply chain (and often across countries and continents). In this instance the system helps us to deliver over 1 million kilograms of air freight per annum, and 3,000 20-foot equivalent units (TEU) per annum, with each shipment crossing the Atlantic from the United States into the United Kingdom before making its way into the retail stores.

What makes this process stand out is the fact that we are able to service stores in the United Kingdom directly from the customer's warehouse in the United States. As a result, the order processing and picking are completed before the cargo is trucked to New York – where we have established guaranteed capacity agreements to fly PMCs direct to Heathrow. Once in the United Kingdom, the freight is cross-docked at both Colnbrook and Lichfield, before our team break down the PMCs, sort into cartons and scan to pallets for final delivery into stores, via an electronic proof of delivery (POD).

The beauty of this system is twofold. The first is the sheer transparency of the system. Because the control tower monitors each milestone within the supply chain from start to finish, the client has full order visibility – including a same-day electronic POD. The second benefit is less about the service, and more about the efficiencies of process. By ordering and picking in the United Kingdom and then delivering direct to stores, the company has made the usual freight process significantly leaner, effectively eliminating the need for a large warehouse and staff (and all the overheads that this would entail). Taken together, this means a better service for the customers, at a better overall cost/margin to us as the provider. That said, to get to a point whereby the interests of both provider and client merge like this requires an awful lot of progressive investment in the latest technology and software – so it's not necessarily as easy as it sounds.

But what I think is most interesting about this particular client service is the way that it can be seen as a timely microcosm of the ways that air freight is evolving, and will continue to evolve in the future. For example, this service embeds e-commerce and e-freight into the day-to-day operations, which is symptomatic of the way in which technology has fundamentally altered, and streamlined, logistics. Clearly, technology is no longer the coming force – it is here, useable and already creating a significant impact.

However, I think it is really important to point out that this technology, and indeed any further advancements that may be introduced over the coming decade, will never replace the value of a personal service and a strong working relationship. As long as there are humans involved (and hopefully we've got a good while yet until the robots take over!) then there will always be the need for the comforts of personal advice, knowledge and assurance – and I think that the best freight forwarders, whether air, sea or road, understand that. After all, before your technology can demonstrate exactly how brilliant your service is, you need to have established the trust of your customer. Likewise, if there are issues – and we all know that no technology is infallible – it makes a huge difference if you have a positive personal relationship with your client to fall back on.

The other interesting thing about this example is that it reveals another increasingly important aspect of modern freight – the fact that it is often intermodal. In an ever more globalized world economy, clients and companies have ever more specific and demanding logistical needs. Naturally, that calls for ever more expansive solutions – so having air, road and sea capability (and the ability to combine them) is a real advantage. To use the client case in point, for all of the innovative interactivity and technology on offer, this system simply wouldn't be anywhere near as effective if there wasn't such harmony between the modes of transport; between air freight (and in this instance, sometimes ocean freight too) and the road freight that sandwiches it on either side of the Atlantic. Being able to use each mode to whichever extent is needed means that the whole operation can be truly optimized and that considerations of speed, efficiency and cost can be delicately balanced.

(For more information on Hellmann Worldwide Logistics, visit **www.hellmann.net**; to follow Hellmann on Twitter go to **www.twitter.com/HellmannUK**.)

Cool logistics

08

This chapter discusses some of the different products that are classified as perishables, including fruit and vegetables, flowers and plants, fish and live seafood, animal products, medicines and pharmaceuticals. All these products must be kept at lower temperatures than normal in order to maintain their quality. These temperatures vary depending on the item. It is a sector that demands great skill and which operates under strict international regulations.

The cool chain

Sebastiaan Scholte, President of the Cool Chain Association and CEO of Jan de Rijk Logistics, summarizes the scope of this sector:

> Perishable products account for more than 10 per cent of total shipments by air and are more seasonal than general cargo, making it difficult to optimize capacity all year long. Consumers and commodity markets define the price ceiling for final consumer price therefore most products cannot absorb higher transport costs. Due to the nature of most perishable products, there are directional imbalances of air cargo trade in most export markets. The industry is experiencing modal shift as new container technology comes on stream, largely driven by costs. Another factor for growers and shippers is the impact of weather, which clearly does not affect the pharma sector. Then there is the problem of claims, which can hit the bottom line. Largest perishable trade flows are at geographical proximity – Africa-Europe, South America-United States, Intra Asia and for basic perishables it is demographics rather than economics that define growth.

Part of daily life

The demand for the transport and delivery of large quantities of fresh produce and medicines from around the world has become an accepted feature of daily life in most developed societies and is mostly taken for granted by the public. In supermarkets and pharmacies throughout affluent economies everywhere, people expect to have access to out-of-season fruit such as mangos, vegetables such as asparagus, roses for Valentine's Day and safe medication. Over the last 20 years, a new industry has been developed to supply this demand. However, maintaining the freshness of the fruit and flowers and the integrity of pharmaceuticals presents a huge challenge to the suppliers, transporters, airports, handlers and distributors. These special supply chains must maintain and secure every link to the same impeccable standards throughout varying levels of temperatures, conditions, facilities and knowledge. The creation of systems and technologies that protect the products has evolved into what is collectively known as 'the cool chain'. The logistics industry describes perishables as being shipments that, due to their nature, will spoil without proper care and handling. This includes, but is not limited to, fresh produce, seafood, floral products, fruits, berries and live tropical fish, medicines, drugs, cosmetics and some electronic elements.

Market fluctuations

Within the cool chain logistics sector, competition is always fierce with an element of risk. Because the harvesting of some produce can be irregular or seasonal, market conditions and prices can vary considerably. This means that business planning contains a strong element of unreliability. The margins may be very tight and thus short-term losses can be easily suffered which impact directly on long-term viability. Companies working in these perishable markets, however, know their business well and based on years of experience are able to sustain worthwhile profits.

On the other hand most pharmaceutical products are required and supplied on a more constant and sustainable basis, with less price fluctuation throughout the supply chain to the point of delivery. Pharmaceutical products need to maintain an absolutely constant temperature throughout their complete supply chain cycle and they are transported in specially developed containers with a constant temperature that can be individually set between $-20°C$ and $+20°C$. Despite the improvements that have been introduced over the last two decades, loss of product quality can be between 20 and 30 per cent, often due to poor handling on the tarmac, damage to pallets, delays to flights, etc. The industry needs a new approach to cooperation between the carriers, the forwarders, the handlers and truckers in order to streamline the perishables traffic. The air cargo operators really need to learn from the integrators for this.

Creating standards

To most people, out-of-season asparagus, strawberries for Christmas or insulin injections just come from shops or from the supermarket. But, behind the scenes, the logistics industry provides the vital link in the process backed by the necessary management and control systems, refrigerated transport and warehousing, which together complete the cool chain. While a large proportion of perishables are moved by sea, it is the air freight sector upon which many of these more time-sensitive and high-value products depend.

In 2003, the different players working in the perishables sector agreed that there was a pressing need to establish a global structure of industry standards and rules. From this meeting the Cool Chain Association was created. Now well established, it works closely with bodies such as IATA and TIACA in establishing industry standards and criteria and to promote more efficient perishable supply chains.

Since then, there has been an enormous investment on the part of operators in an effort to maintain high standards, provide cheaper safer transportation for perishables at low cost while reducing the impact on the environment. Considerable benefits pass to the local growers and their employees in some parts of the developing world from their ability to air freight valuable consignments of perishables to eager consumer markets in more wealthy countries. Kenya is a good example of this. The flower trade is one of the country's leading sources of foreign revenue, employing many who process and pack cut flowers for vital export revenue. This is happening in many countries in Africa, Central and South America with high rates of unemployment and is providing jobs. Fresh salad crops and green vegetables are also important exports from these countries. They provide year-round fresh produce for consumption throughout the industrialized communities of the world. Similarly, asparagus earns a great deal of export revenue for Peru, which is currently the world's largest single exporter, earning more than US$400 million a year and employing thousands of workers. Logistics companies and sea and air carriers have developed very effective and cost-efficient techniques and equipment for handling this traffic.

The cool chain business

The business is an unbroken chain with controlled temperature conditions to ensure the integrity of shipments of fresh fish, cut flowers or dairy products. The operators are working closely with specialist equipment makers to find newer and better ways of keeping these products at the right temperature throughout the chain. While there are many who argue against the merits of global transport of perishables, the fact remains that it is far less polluting than growing the same items in northern climates. Sebastiaan Scholte of the Cool Chain Association states that although many attempts have been made to establish growing facilities in Holland, for example, the results have been disappointing and expensive. Dutch exporter Levaart reports that much of the traditional production of vegetables such as bell peppers has been transferred to more cost-effective climates. Production in colder climates is very expensive, largely due to high fuel, heating and labour costs, and creates more emissions. Furthermore, in the developing world, people depend on this trade for their livelihood and have the climate to grow crops naturally. The ethics and moral arguments are a subject of discussion in the context of the world's need to grow more food and cut down on waste and spoilage by exposure to high temperatures.

The business is broadly divided into the following:

- food products – fruit, vegetables, live fish and shellfish, meat and meat products;
- fresh flowers and plants;
- medical products – pharmaceuticals, vaccines, body parts, plasma; and
- live insects and mammals, bull semen, eggs.

In the following section, we present a few examples of products being transported within the cool chain. The sheer volume of products involved makes it impossible to include all, but the important message is that all grown produce has a very limited shelf life and rapid delivery without damage or spoilage is vital for growers, retailers, carriers and logistics companies. For the pharma business, although it is easier overall to work within specified temperature environments, strict and accurate cool chain control is essential to guarantee quality.

Flowers

Despite a severe worldwide recession and other social problems that have occurred over the last 20 years, the market for fresh flowers has remained healthy. While flowers could be classed as a luxury by some, individuals and companies continue to spend money on flowers and plants. Celebrations such as St Valentine's and Mother's Day more than treble the usual demand. In addition, weddings, funerals and hotel displays ensure the steady stream of flowers. However, this is a highly complex and cost-conscious market where failure to protect the integrity of the supply chain can result in poor shelf life and retail performance, resulting in heavy losses.

In 1995, I visited a leading rose farm near Bogota in Columbia. The proprietor complained bitterly that despite the outstanding quality of the roses and the care spent packaging them in flat cardboard cartons, when they were delivered to the airport they were carelessly stacked 20 boxes or more high and left out in the heat and frequent rain storms until they eventually were loaded onto freighter aircraft. She pointed out that the bottom layers were invariably crushed, resulting in considerable losses and wastage.

Since that time, the national business has revolutionized its working practices and facilities to become a top accredited industry. Florverde, established in 1996 by the Columbian flower growers association (Asocolflores), set standards and accreditation programmes now recognized worldwide as a high-quality benchmark. Today, over 170 farms have been awarded the quality certificate and flower exports amount to over 500,000 tons per year. The airline Lan Chile has installed a 2,000 square metre warehouse to ensure that throughput and reduced truck waiting times are as efficient as possible.

The main flower exporters in Latin America are Colombia and Ecuador. For both countries, floriculture is a fundamental part of the economy. Colombia's agricultural exports include coffee and bananas but the country is the leading exporter of flowers from Latin America. It has about 7,000 hectares of different types, most importantly roses, carnations, and chrysanthemums. The main export growers are located near the capital Bogota and the Rionegra area. Colombia is the second largest producer of cut flowers after the Netherlands. The trade employs between 150 and 200,000 workers accounting for over 5 per cent of the country's GDP. The United States is the biggest customer for the flowers, with the EU second. The airport of El Dorado is modern, well equipped and capable of dealing with the flowers in a cool 2,000+ square metre warehouse operated by Linea Aerea de Colombia, the local affiliate of LAN Cargo.

Ecuador is the second largest flower exporter in the region, with about 4,000 hectares, with 2,500 dedicated to roses. The provinces where floriculture is centred are Pichincha, Cotopaxi, Imbabura and Azuay.

Kenya

Agriculture contributes around 25 per cent of GDP and is one of the top foreign exchange earners for the country. Kenya is a main exporter of cut flowers to the EU, with a market share of about 38 per cent. Approximately

65 per cent of exported flowers are sold through the Dutch auctions at Aalsmeer. Japan, Russia and the United States are also important markets. According to Ron Boss of Hilverda De Boer, a leading flower exporter based next to the Aalsmeer auctions, there is a growing trend for producers to deal directly with big retail outlets and avoid sending the produce to auction in Holland. The biggest attraction to buying in Holland, however, is the enormous range of around 25,000 varieties of flowers and plants to be found in one place.

Although many flowers and plants are flown directly into each European country, a large percentage of flowers and plants are traded through the Flora Holland auctions at Aalsmeer, Bleiswiujk, Eelde, Naaldwijk and Rijnsburg in the Netherlands. Flowers and plants are delivered from all over the world for the daily auctions, which supply wholesale florists and traders throughout Europe. This is the largest flower auction in the world whose building covers 990,000 square metres (10.6 million square feet, 243 acres). Flowers from all over the world are traded daily. Around 20 million flowers are sold each day with a 15 per cent increase around special days such as Valentine's Day and Mother's Day.

The United States

The growing demand for cut flowers and plants in the United States is supplied globally. Although many flights, especially from Latin America, serve major cities directly, the biggest flower market is based in Los Angeles. While California itself supplies many types of flowers and plants, especially sunflowers and lilies, unfortunately, due to several years of severe water shortages, Californian growers of flowers and fruits are having to switch to other crops needing less water. Flowers coming from South America include carnations and roses flown in from Chile. Supplies also come from around the world, for example, chrysanthemums and roses from Kenya, the Canary Islands, Italy and India; orchids from Thailand and proteas and roses from South Africa.

Despite the technical advances in cool chain equipment and containers that are attracting more perishables to ocean freight, it would be impossible to operate this vast global industry without the use of air freight logistics.

Fruit and vegetables

Most countries are able to successfully farm and deliver crops to wholesalers, stores and supermarkets within their own national markets. However, despite much ill-informed protest about unnecessary emissions caused by air and sea freight, it is often more efficient and cheaper to fly produce to markets. Some produce has become very popular and is thus flown where road transport takes too much time. The markets in Holland are again a vital link in the fruit and flower trade in Europe. According to Johan Littel of Levarht, a leading trader in these commodities, Holland still produces a significant amount of tomatoes, bell peppers and other vegetables but production has shifted to other area such as New Zealand where production continues in the southern summer. Between the two locations, the company is able to maintain constant shipment to customers in the Far East.

Asparagus

Asparagus was traditionally a short-season luxury vegetable in Europe and North America but thanks to international trade in this product, it is now available all year round and is no longer considered as a luxury food. The production of asparagus has become the main agricultural high-value export by air from Peru, one of the most important producers and exporters of this crop worldwide. While the largest overall producer of asparagus is China, Peru is the largest and principal exporter of fresh green asparagus, exporting mostly to the United States and Europe. Other markets such as Australia and Asia have important seasonal demands. Peru benefits from the advantages of an ideal climate and geographical location producing high year-round yields.

Fish and live seafood

The availability of fish is impacted by overfishing, which has resulted in fishing fleets operating at greater distances to try to locate less-fished areas. If trawlers continue to take smaller fish, often to convert them to fertilizer or animal feed, eventually the marine food chain will collapse. Fish farming is one solution and in countries such as Norway, farmed salmon is a huge export commodity, especially to Russia. Altogether, Norway is the world's biggest fish farmer and accounts for about 50 per cent of the global salmon trade, well ahead of world number two, Chile. The sector exports nearly US$1 billion of seafood each month.

Iceland is also a big producer of fresh fish and exports. Most of the fish transported by air goes to Europe, but exports to the United States have doubled since 2011. Iceland is also famous for its freshwater fish; trout, arctic char and particularly salmon. There is a salmon river that runs right through the middle of Reykjavik! Many of the fish factories are close to the airport, convenient for exporters to have the fish processed, packed and brought to the airport for transport within 48 hours from the time it was caught. Sustainable fish stocks and good treatment of the marine ecosystem help to maintain the steady trade.

CASE STUDY   The Fish Society goes global

The Fish Society is a small internet fishmonger based in the UK. It sells 250 kinds of fish – all frozen. Importantly, its customer base comprises individuals, not restaurants: The Fish Society supplies people who want to eat top-quality fish *at home*. Therefore orders tend to be smaller and the cost of shipment is always significant.

The Fish Society necessarily operates at the top of the market. As founder James Smith says, 'There's no point in a customer opening our expensively packaged and shipped box and being disappointed with the content. Our customers are looking for wild salmon, not farmed salmon. They want diver-caught scallops. They pay top dollar for prawns you eat with two hands.'

The Fish Society first experimented with foreign shipments in 2009. Step one was to hire an IATA-registered training company to deliver a course in packing fish with dry ice for air freight. (Dry ice is used every day in the UK; by road it is not a dangerous good.) Step two was to obtain an approval from its shipping company to put dry ice into air freighted parcels. This required six sign-offs, which took weeks to obtain.

The first parcel it sent arrived back two days later together with a rejection notice in which the inspector pointed out that the dry ice label was on the wrong face of the box. The fee for the inspection was US$40 – nobody had mentioned that. A week later, another shipment simply missed a connection, resulting in two very unhappy customers. It all seemed like an expensive – but fortunately small – disaster. The Fish Society had more urgent issues to deal with: foreign shipments were suspended.

It was three years before the next attempt came about. A customer in France placed a US$700 order. In fact, she placed two. The first was simply ignored – partly because the payment hadn't gone through, and partly because, says Smith: 'We thought it was a wind-up. Our offering is streets ahead of UK supermarket fish. But the gap against French supermarket fish is a lot narrower. We couldn't imagine anyone in France being seriously interested in our fish.' How wrong can you be? Even French supermarkets don't offer wild Scottish salmon.

Three months later the same person placed a further order. 'So we picked up the phone and said, "We'd love to send your order but the delivery surcharge will be US$180" (it was a very large order). She said "Fine." So we sent it and started to re-evaluate foreign deliveries. And how we could we make them work second time around?'

The first thing The Fish Society did was to reduce expectations. Their 'UK-delivered mindset' was that the fish must arrive frozen. But they decided they could not offer this assurance abroad without incurring the massive extra costs of using dry ice. So the dry ice was dropped. Says Smith, 'We just used gel ice – no labels, no inspections, no rejections. We told the customer their fish would arrive cold, not frozen.'

This did not solve the problem of missed connections or the problem of two-day transit times for remote locations. The discovery that 'next day' was not available to much of rural France and quite a bit of Switzerland was an essential if hard step forward. The delivery advice was revised, simply to state that deliveries were allowed to be one day late without recourse. And the quantity of gel ice packed in each was lifted to cope with extended transit times.

Still, there were problems. One day late was ok; two days was not. The Fish Society was using an intermediary to ship via a big brand courier. According to Smith, 'The big brand just wasn't interested in our business. Their rates were terrible, although we didn't realize quite how terrible at the time. Eventually the intermediary turned up and offered us prices not much more than half those which we were paying.' But the intermediary took The Fish Society a step away from the courier and proved unable to get the courier's attention when there was a delivery hiccup. So it was back to the courier. Eventually some sensible rates were forthcoming and calls in pursuit of late deliveries began to get attention.

Foreign interest began to pick up. UK expats in Hong Kong just can't find smoked haddock. And The Fish Society found its next blind alley. Unbeatable rates from a specialist Far Eastern courier were very alluring until it emerged that their 'next day' started to be counted the day after the parcel was collected.

James Smith sums up The Fish Society's experience so far:

Highly perishable shipments like ours, in need of refrigeration but only receiving it from within the parcel itself, and where the cost of shipment is being met by a retail customer, create headaches for everyone involved. It's always tempting to blame the courier. But the fact is, the buck stops with you. It's your parcel, your customer, your business.

For beginners like us, there was no way to address these problems other than to experience them all one by one and then adapt to customers' expectations. We can now read between the lines of the courier's parcel tracking platform. We know the difference between 'scanned for shipment' and 'awaiting shipment'. We also know when the courier is building in some margin. Last week we shipped a parcel to Sydney. As we had expected, it arrived a day ahead of the scheduled delivery and despite spending 30 hours of transit time in the tropics, it arrived at 3 degrees centigrade. The customer was delighted.

This example demonstrates the inventiveness and innovation that are in daily practice in the perishables sector.

Another factor affecting sales of edible fresh fish and seafood is transport costs. Long distance deliveries by air have been badly affected by fluctuations in oil prices. A good example is Spain, which is the second biggest consumer nation for fresh fish after Japan. In the 1980s and 1990s frequent regular freighter loads of fresh fish were being flown into Spain, as well as other European main hubs – Paris, London and Frankfurt. The merluza (hake), a special favourite in Spain, was imported from South Africa and Chile, with lobsters from Canada. Two factors – recession and high fuel costs – hit a weakening demand, resulting in a drastic reduction in this trade in Spain. The airports in northern Spain such as Vitoria and Zaragoza were, at their peak in the late 1990s, handling several full freighters of fresh fish every week. Today, any fish shipments arrive in other airport hubs – Paris, London and Amsterdam – and are moved by truck to other markets.

Imported seafood products

China is the largest producer of seafood products in the world, and Japan and the United States are the largest importers. Over three-quarters of the seafood consumed in the United States is imported from other countries. In 2009, 5.5 billion pounds of edible fish products valued at US$14.8 billion were imported into the United States. Shrimp is the most important imported seafood product, and over 1.2 billion pounds of shrimp were imported in 2010. Thailand was the leading United States supplier of shrimp followed by Ecuador, Indonesia, China, Vietnam and Mexico. Tuna was the second most important imported product in 2010, and almost equal amounts of canned, fresh and frozen tuna were imported that year. Major suppliers of canned tuna are Thailand, Philippines, Indonesia, Vietnam and Ecuador. Other important products in order of volume imported include: salmon from Norway, Canada, and Chile; ground fish species like cod, haddock, pollock and hake from Canada and Northern Europe; crabs and crabmeat from Southeast Asia; and frozen fish blocks used to make fish portions and sticks from China, Russia, Canada and Iceland.

CASE STUDY Live lobster Clearwater perspective

Live lobster has three key criteria that must be met to ensure a successful shipment: temperature, time and handling; they are premium-quality lobsters.

Lobsters are poikilotherms, taking on the varied body temperatures of their changing environment, and their metabolism is governed by body temperature. Low temperature maintains slow metabolism, which is key to a lobster being able to survive out of water for extended periods. High temperatures increase metabolism and therefore oxygen demand that cannot be met by their inefficient aquatic gills while out of water. Although lobsters can be found in aquatic habitats in which the water temperature ranges from just above freezing to as high as 25°C, out-of-water temperatures above 5°C reduce their survival time to below 24 hours and arrival condition post-consignment is not consistent with expectations for a high-quality, strong, fresh lobster.

With ideal temperature conditions, lobsters can be shipped out of water for up to 48 hours with little to no mortality. Beyond 48 hours, post-shipment mortality increases exponentially with each additional hour out of water. This 48-hour shipment time is why air freight is necessary to allow live lobsters to reach far-off international destinations while maintaining their premium quality and strength. However, since cold chain logistics within and between airlines is inconsistent at best, and non-existent in most cases, lobsters must be packed in heavily insulated shipping boxes with self-contained frozen gel ice packs to maintain the ideal 3–5°C temperature inside the box during air shipment. Ice pack quantity is adjusted seasonally and by destination; for example, air temperatures up to 30°C have been measured during the Canadian portion of air freight consignments. Significant expenditure is put into highly insulated, non-recyclable extruded polystyrene materials such as Styrofoam as well as gel ice packs that can comprise as much as 22 per cent of the shipped box weight, adding significant shipment costs and inefficiencies. This system contrasts with ground transportation that has much better cold chain logistics with little break in the cold chain parameters for the duration of the consignment. However, ground transportation is too slow and therefore only feasible for domestic, local shipments.

Product handling is the third criterion and has a significant effect on the success of a live lobster shipment. Lobsters that are packed for air travel and left in a cooler on a shelf undisturbed can live for up to 120 hours. However, lobsters are sensitive to movements and forces that they do not normally experience while in the aquatic world in which buoyancy negates any gravitational forces that are experienced while out of water. Rough handling of a box of packed lobsters, and vibrations from constant movement or jostling during transport, cause the lobster's metabolism to increase above normal levels and shorten the survival time out of water. There is a direct effect of degree of rough handling and post-shipment mortality, therefore training on proper handling of the boxes of live lobsters is key to a successful air shipment programme. It is for this reason that Clearwater has developed a lobster university programme to educate all those who handle lobsters or boxes of lobsters on the effects of mishandling and to teach all staff including lobster packers, truck drivers, air cargo handlers and couriers on the proper technique and environment for successful live lobster shipping.

Supply chain, cold chain and transport

There are several challenges to seafood exporters when using air transport. Exporters that operate in small markets, such as seafood exporters from Atlantic Canada, have limited cargo transport options. Canada has historically small narrow-body aircraft for passenger flights, and very few cargo-specific offerings. This leads to extreme competition for limited cargo lift, and trucking seafood to larger urban centres to find wide-body or cargo flights. The trucking and extra handling that occur have a negative impact on the arrival quality of a commodity like live lobsters. The need to truck from small markets also limits the air options that can be used as the lobsters have already spent several hours out of water. Every year about 3.7 million kg of live lobsters leave the Canadian coast of Nova Scotia to end up on European plates. About 2 million kg or 55 per cent of all these exports to Europe pass through Brussels airport.

Ground handling is also very important when it comes to live lobster shipments. Extended time on the tarmac negatively impacts the quality. Exposure to heat stresses the lobsters, and exposure to rain damages the cartons and ultimately affects the arrival condition of the lobsters. Proper ground handling procedures, like quickly moving the lobsters to a cooler until loading time, will improve the chances of strong healthy products at arrival. The trend is to design aircraft to carry more passengers than before, which means that there is more cargo space taken up per flight. Limited cargo lift on a narrow body becomes tighter than ever.

Of all modes of transport, air transport is the likeliest to incur shipment delays or cancellations. Cargo booking cancellations and delays are usually due to weather events, but there are also cancellations and delays due to mechanical or crew issues, higher than expected cargo weight, balancing due to heavy fuel requirements, etc. When these events occur at a secondary point where lobster has been trucked, there are often limited options to rebook, or return by air. Sometimes returning by road transport is the only way.

While there have been different product offerings over the years on the cold chain side of cargo, they have mainly been far too expensive for the competitive lobster market. With the trend towards airlines utilizing shorter-range cargo planes, which means more transfers during a single consignment, the limits of handling, time out of water and the typically uncontrolled cold chain are pushing the limits of live lobster shipment programmes. Considerable expense in high-priced packaging, gel ice packs and temperature monitors for airline consignments limits the success and profitability of a potentially lucrative and growing business.

Insects and eggs

Certain living creatures are accepted by air carriers, in special packs. These include destroyers of noxious pests and other insects sent to or from officially recognized institutions, leeches and certain parasites, and silkworms. In addition the following may be sent to some destinations: caterpillars, earthworms, fish fry and eggs, lugworms, maggots, mealworms, pupae, chrysalides and rag worms. Large quantities of insects such as grasshoppers are sent for zoos for feeding some animals and birds. Bees are now being moved to help with fruit production in some countries where there have been problems with diseases and predators. Air transport is usually necessary due to the short time involved.

Animal semen

For the artificial insemination of (mostly farm) animals, special containers have been designed which allow the transport of frozen or liquid semen. With liquid nitrogen as coolant, the product can be kept without harm for several days, depending on the amount of coolant. Some containers need to be returned to origin for reuse, an expensive process, but new types of disposable containers are now available, a much cheaper option. These containers can pass through X-ray scanners without harming the contents, which are not classified as dangerous goods.

Pharmaceuticals

This is the biggest and most profitable single sector in the growing cool chain market and the most temperature sensitive. The health and survival of many thousands depend on getting vaccines, insulin, blood plasma and other temperature-sensitive healthcare products. In the words of Sebastiaan Scholte, Chairman of the Cool Chain Association: 'There is a desperate need for standardization in handling pharmaceutical and healthcare products. Poor communication and training, skill deficiency plus cost pressures are affecting quality of service.' As much as 15–20 per cent of transported products are wasted and have to be discarded at the point of delivery. Maintaining the integrity of the cool chain for this estimated US$950 billion global pharmaceutical industry is a constant challenge.

The industry's biggest challenge is delivering products and vaccines in perfect condition to the consumer. Shippers have raised concerns about the supply chain's integrity and generally agreed that cutting costs was putting this under considerable strain. The manufacturers of pharmaceutical products are responsible for their products being in perfect condition, but the lack of specialized skills and training within the cool chain is one of the factors causing problems, along with a lack of transparency and communication.

The exposure of all perishable products, especially pharma, to high temperatures continues to result in substantial loss of usable products at the delivery point. Sebstiaan Scholte comments that currently losses are running high and the airlines, logistics companies and handlers need to work closer together to improve this situation. This problem of temperature extremes, coupled with solar radiation, is causing some manufacturers to abandon the speed of air transport for the slower, but less volatile, sea freight. At some airports such as Liège in Belgium, and at Findel Airport in Luxembourg, special equipment that protects the shipment on the tarmac enables rapid transfers from aircraft to warehouse. Such facilities are required at any airport handling pharma shipments.

To make matters more difficult, some biological medicines and drugs are not only temperature-sensitive but are also liable to damage from violent movement and vibration. This puts even more pressure on the container manufacturers, handlers and airlines. Whereas a large proportion of manufactured pharma products are destined for countries with cool chain facilities, there is also a large and regrettably growing need for these life-saving products in the many regions of the world suffering from conflict, disasters, famine and starvation. To deliver such sensitive drugs and vaccines in perfect condition (2–8°C) to areas with no suitable cooling facilities is a monumental challenge facing aid workers such as MSF and Save the Children, working in extreme heat and usually in inaccessible places. In these cases there is frequently a long journey over bad roads, which tests the ingenuity of the logistics companies.

Healthcare products, traditionally manufactured and exported from Switzerland, Germany, the United Kingdom and the United States, have also become a growth industry in China, Russia, South Korea and Mexico. Thanks to the diminishing margins of the products in a highly competitive sector, plus low-cost generic versions, more and more companies are switching to the cheaper option of ocean freight, but air freight remains the default choice for speed. There has been a lot of interest in pharmaceutical shipments in the air freight industry in recent years as airlines and forwarders search for traffic that can give them those elusive higher yields: some 30 airlines now offer services for pharmaceutical products and many are investing in expanding their cool chain facilities.

The Swedish cool chain logistics specialist Envirotainer is one company playing an important role in the transportation of pharmaceuticals with its range of active temperature-controlled air cargo containers that it rents to users when they are required. As long as the refrigerants, usually dry ice, are maintained and the batteries are powered, the temperature can be maintained as needed – no matter how long the journey, or whether cooling or heating is required.

Envirotainer's active temperature control technology consists of a ULD container made out of high-performance insulation material, with an internal fan and sensor. Warm air drawn into the sealed container by the fan passes over dry ice in a separate compartment and is cooled before being guided back out to the loading area. This convection process promotes a constant, regulated environment providing a stable pre-set temperature for up to 72 hours. The internal sensor helps keep the temperature within the required limits, which can range from –20°C to +20°C, depending on the product. United States-based CSafe is a similar company to Envirotainer and also provides a cold chain air transport container that meets the temperature and regulatory requirements for pharmaceutical cold chain management.

Even if handling and quality standards are uniform throughout the world, shippers, freight forwarders and the cargo-carrying airlines need specially trained and certified staff to handle pharmaceutical products and get them to their destination in impeccable condition. Envirotainer has a Qualified Envirotainer Provider (QEP) programme, which acknowledges service providers that meet the strict requirements of its Training and Quality Programme for Good Distribution Practices guidance documents, including the requirements of the Parenteral Drug Association (PDA) and the International Air Transport Association (IATA).

The industry is bombarded with regulations and directives, most of them issued over the past decade. It is an area full of acronyms and organizations – the FDA, the EU, the MHRA, the WHO, the PDA – that attempt to define the way pharmaceuticals should be handled and transported. For example, new EU guidelines (EU343/01) state that pharmaceutical shippers have to submit to a transport qualification, part of which is that they have to audit whether airlines can really do what they say they can. Investment in training, equipment and different processes are required.

Dangerous goods in pharma

Many goods used in biotechnology and pharmaceuticals are potentially hazardous, so everyone working in the distribution chain must guarantee that the goods are properly labelled, packaged and handled, and that documentation is correct and follows IATA regulations.

IATA publishes a manual for the shipping of perishables including pharmaceuticals, the Perishable Cargo Regulations (PCR). The PCR provides access to the most current and efficient practices for perishable cargo operations and an integral tool to achieve cost savings and avoid delays by guaranteeing shipments are problem-free and compliant with international or local regulations. The PCR is a necessity for everyone involved in the transport of perishable goods by air, specifically commercial shippers, shippers of fresh fruits and flowers, pharmaceutical companies, ground handlers, freight forwarders and airlines.

Ground handling

To protect sensitive products from temperature fluctuations during offloading and transportation to the warehouse, fast unloading or loading is essential as direct sunlight can quickly damage most products. In some airports such as Dubai, specially designed 'Cool dollies' ferry pallets to and from cool rooms in airport warehouses, also operated under the same stringent guidelines.

It is during loading and unloading of trucks and aircraft that the cool chain is most likely to be broken. If products such as pharmaceuticals are moved in temperature-controlled containers, this problem does not occur but in countries where fresh produce or flowers are loaded, there can be the risk of exposure to heat, which will damage the goods and their shelf life.

Conclusions

With some exceptions, importing fresh produce by sea freight from tropical countries to markets in Europe and North America with 10–20 days' lead time is not an option. In these situations, northern European and US consumers will always be reliant on produce delivered by air. Customers demand fresh out-of-season and exotic produce or have to rely on frozen produce. Most people now have the appetite and taste for products that years ago would never have been available. Pharmaceutical products demand 100 per cent control and companies involved in this business keep striving for new standards of excellence. The technology of the cool chain sector is constantly evolving.

Express
and mail

09

Worldwide air freight tonnages over the last two to three decades indicate the growing strength of the express operators over conventional air cargo carriers. The global companies now leading this business are known as 'integrators' thanks to their fully integrated in-house systems covering every aspect of the business or small freighter operator with relevant traffic rights. They collect shipments, control and deliver them, totally within their own systems, backed by a reliable tracking service for their customers. With large fleets of freight aircraft, the integrators are not affected by the restrictions or timetables of scheduled passenger flights and are able to concentrate totally on these shipments. In the case of deliveries to destinations with potentially low volumes where a regular rotation is not justified, cargo is often allocated to another carrier that covers the route. Conventional airlines, obliged to compete with their more streamlined integrator competitors, have in many ways caught up with these methods and technologies; they now offer excellent services, but must always look after their priority passengers. The same also applies to normal cargo flown in their bellies. Many of the systems employed by airlines and handlers are derived from the leading integrators. The carriage of post was the original base of the fledgling air cargo industry and has continued as an important part of the cargo business. However, with the revolution in e-mail, traffic of conventional letters has been replaced by online trading of consumer goods (see Chapter 13).

In the 1960s international postal services were generally slow and unreliable and as a result businesses often preferred to pay for a premium service from an express operator. In the United States, Federal Express, thanks to considerable promotion, became a household word and people would be heard to say, 'I will FedEx the documents.' It was a clever move to promote the service direct to the people in offices, especially secretaries and receptionists who could choose the service for urgent items.

The world's postal authorities realized that they were rapidly losing business. In his book *The Rise of Global Delivery Services*, James Campbell

(2001, J Campbell Press) provides a detailed account of how post offices in the 1980s developed services to compete with privately owned integrators. An excellent example is the action by the French post office in 1986: a joint venture with a private airline TAT was formed (SFMI). It was able to operate as a private company while retaining the solid public service base. Since that time the industrialized nations have developed systems that allow them not only to compete with the express operators but also to cooperate with them. In Germany the Bundespost was privatized in 1995 and today Deutsche Post DHL employs around half a million people in over 220 countries. It has become the world's largest logistics operator, involved in all aspects of supply chain activities.

Overall in Europe, the express industry employs around 300,000 people and delivers more than 260 million packages each year – almost half of the intra-Europe air cargo market. The express delivery companies are able to connect 90 per cent of the world economy within 72 hours. In 2009, the industry had a direct employment base of around 1.3 million staff worldwide, providing work for people with a wide range of skills including sorting and delivering, administration and sales, as well as engineers/technicians and managers. It is estimated that the express industry has also created a total of 2.75 million jobs worldwide through indirect employment.

Market sectors

The express industry's biggest markets are IT and telecommunications, aviation, pharmaceuticals, electronics, retail, and financial and business services, and now the rapidly expanding e-tailing sector. The industry:

- operates in over 220 countries;
- handles over 6 million packages daily;
- operates and owns more than 1,200 aircraft and loads shipments on over 2,000 commercial flights daily;
- operates 200,000 trucks and delivery vehicles;
- operates global electronic track and trace systems;
- is now used as default transport by virtually all multinational companies.

Changes in trading patterns

Thanks to the burgeoning online retail sector, almost all goods – electronics, fashion, DVDs, food and pharmaceuticals – are regularly purchased by this method. While retailers may be suffering, courier companies and express operators in all developed countries benefit from this trend. An estimated 40 to 50 per cent of businesses now rely on this overnight delivery revolution. World trade is forecast to increase by over 60 per cent between 2008 and 2018 despite the recession of 2008/9. Many companies state that productivity and reduced costs can be achieved by using express delivery. The air cargo industry is now better equipped to attack the market by the use of thousands of international wide-body flights with vastly increased cargo capacity.

Integrators

An integrator is so named as it handles its traffic almost entirely through its own internal systems and controls, although it frequently subcontracts other carriers when necessary. Since their introduction, integrators have become one of the main competitors to traditional air cargo operators. At the same time, however, thanks to subcontracting to other airlines and handlers, they have created new cargo for these carriers. The increasing use of sea freight is also eating into traditional air traffic. The United States-based integrators, faced with limited domestic markets, started to expand both their geographical reach and their product portfolios to include more conventional international cargo, utilizing unused aircraft capacity and even branching out into sea freight.

The list of the biggest cargo carrying airlines in 2013 was headed by FedEx with a fleet of 643 aircraft, DHL (250), UPS (237) and TNT (182), followed by Korean Air Cargo (27), China Postal Airlines (22),Cathay Pacific Cargo (22), China Airlines Cargo (21) and Cargolux (20). Although at one time carrying documents and traditional express packages, today these companies compete globally for all categories of air cargo. Brief profiles show the scope and diversification of the leading integrators.

DHL

DHL was founded in San Francisco in 1969 by Adrian Dalsey, Larry Hillblom and Robert Lynn. In 1971 it became the first US air express operator to offer services to Asia, with a service to the Philippines, followed in 1973 with services to Japan, Hong Kong, Singapore and Australia. In 1976, DHL entered the European market and three years later it expanded its operations to include the carriage of parcels in addition to documents.

In 2000 it signed a strategic agreement with Lufthansa Cargo and Japan Airlines whereby each airline took a 25 per cent stake in the company. DHL was acquired by Deutsche Post in July 2002, when the German postal group bought out the minority shareholdings of the two airlines. Deutsche Post today generates annual revenues of more than €51 billion (US$64.25 billion).

DHL Global Mail operates one of the world's largest delivery networks, with 38 sales offices and 28 production centres in five continents serving more than 200 countries. It is used predominantly to deliver mail, hybrid mail and parcels, including business-to-customer (B2C) traffic. It currently claims to have a 14 per cent share of the worldwide mail market and is capable of handling 6 million mail items daily.

Federal Express (FedEx)

Federal Express, founded by Fred Smith, started overnight services in April 1973. Company headquarters were moved to Memphis, a city selected for its convenient location close to the original target market cities, as well as good weather. The airport was also willing to make the necessary improvements for the operation.

Smith identified the tremendous difficulties in getting packages and other air freight delivered within one to two days. This dilemma motivated him to do the necessary research for resolving the inefficient distribution system. This led to the development of the hub-and-spoke system for handling air cargo shipments. FedEx's main hub is in Memphis, while its other major international hubs are at Paris Charles de Gaulle, Dubai and Guangzhou in Southern China.

It is said that FedEx Express invented express distribution and is the industry's global leader, providing rapid, reliable, time-definite delivery to more than 220 countries and territories, connecting markets that comprise more than 90 per cent of the world's gross domestic product within one to three business days. Today FedEx Express has the world's largest all-cargo air fleet, consisting of Boeing 777 freighters and MD-11Fs as well as Airbus A-300F and A-310F aircraft.

FedEx Corporation provides strategic direction and consolidated financial reporting for the operating companies that operate collectively under the FedEx name worldwide: FedEx Express, FedEx Ground, FedEx Freight, FedEx Office, FedEx Custom Critical, FedEx Trade Networks, FedEx Supply Chain Solutions and FedEx Services. In 2006 FedEx Corp acquired ANC Holdings Limited, a UK domestic express transportation company.

UPS

United Parcel Service Inc started life in Seattle in 1907 as a messenger company; it has grown into a multi-billion-dollar corporation with its headquarters in Atlanta, and total revenues of US$53.1 billion. Today UPS is a global company with one of the most recognized and admired brands in the world. UPS is one of the largest express carrier and package delivery companies and is also a leading provider of specialized transportation, logistics, capital, and e-commerce services, managing the flow of goods, funds and information in more than 200 countries and territories worldwide. The company, also known to many as 'Big Brown', due to the distinctive colour logo, employs around 400,000 people and handles around 4 billion packages and documents annually, or 15.8 million packages and documents each day.

TNT

TNT Express is an international courier delivery services company with headquarters in Hoofddorp, Netherlands. The firm has fully owned operations in 65 countries and delivers documents, parcels and pieces of freight to over 200 countries. Formerly an operating division of TNT NV, TNT Express was demerged from its parent company on 26 May 2011, taking a listing on the Euronext Amsterdam Stock Exchange. TNT NV subsequently renamed itself PostNL.

The company operates road and air transportation networks in Europe, the Middle East and Africa, Asia-Pacific and the Americas. It employs 77,000 people and runs a fleet of 30,000 road vehicles and 46 aircraft. TNT Express aircraft operate under the IATA code of TAY (TNT Airways). In April 2015, FedEx bid to purchase TNT for a reported US$4.4 billion. Should this go ahead, it would involve restructuring the two companies' European facilities. (At the time of going to press, this deal is still not 100 per cent confirmed.)

Postal services

Mail delivery and special parcels services are operated in nearly every country in the world, with varying levels of efficiency. National post offices are supplemented by a whole range of courier companies and mail specialists, the majority of which are purely domestic, although many have international capability. It would be impossible within the scope of this chapter to cover this sector in a meaningful way, so we have restricted our comments to the main integrators and some selected specialist companies.

Parcelforce Worldwide

For over 15 years the company has provided a service for British businesses needing to send express packages overseas as well as within the UK. It has a long history as part of the Royal Mail Group. In 1990 Royal Mail Parcels was rebranded Parcelforce, and there was investment in IT and infrastructure, online tracking and the construction of national and international sorting hubs.

Parcelforce Worldwide is part of the Express Mail Service (EMS) network. EMS offers customers services around the globe through its global priority products, with 54 depots across the UK. EMS is an international postal Express Mail Service for documents and merchandise, offered by postal operators of the Universal Postal Union (UPU) – see below.

China Postal Express & Logistics

Approved by the State Council, China Postal Express & Logistics was co-founded by China Post Group and provincial postal companies as a state-owned limited company in June 2010. The company is the largest integrated express and logistics service provider with the longest history of business operation and the widest coverage in China.

China Postal Express & Logistics has 31 subsidiaries, as well as owning China Postal Airlines and China Post Logistics. China Postal Express & Logistics is mainly engaged in domestic express, international express, contract logistics, and LTL.

United States Postal Service (USPS)

Global Express Guaranteed is the fastest USPS international shipping service, with transportation and guaranteed delivery by FedEx Express services. It features date-certain delivery in one to three business days to more than 190 countries with a money-back guarantee to all destinations.

Operating facilities include 1,250 stations (640 inside the United States, 610 elsewhere) and 12 air express hubs. The international hubs are located in the Asia-Pacific region, EMEA (Europe, Middle East and Africa), Canada and Latin America/Caribbean. FedEx also has 690 world service centres, 1,750 office locations, 6,300 authorized ship centres and alliance partners, and 37,000 drop boxes.

Universal Postal Union (UPU)

The UPU is an intergovernmental organization that provides a forum for governments, postal organizations and other stakeholders in the worldwide postal sector. It works to establish the rules for international mail exchanges among its 191 members and to improve the quality of service for customers. The UPU was created in 1874, initially under the name 'General Postal Union', before changing its name to 'Universal Postal Union' four years later. The UPU established that:

- There should be a uniform flat rate to mail a letter anywhere in the world.
- Postal authorities should give equal treatment to foreign and domestic mail.
- Each country should retain all money it has collected for international postage.

The UPU became a specialized agency of the UN in 1948 and, in 1969, the UPU introduced 'terminal fees' – a new system of payment whereby fees were payable between countries according to the difference in the total weight of mail between them. This new system was fairer when traffic was heavier in one direction than the other.

The EMS Cooperative (Express Mail Service) was created in 1998 within the framework of the UPU. Its main objective is to promote cooperation between members to allow them to provide customers with a high-quality, competitive EMS service worldwide. Today 177 postal administrations have joined the cooperative E-Parcel Group (EPG) network, ideally suited for B2C and C2C deliveries across Europe, through the use of postal administrations.

Conclusions

The entire world logistics industry is liable to rapid and frequent change but the need to transport goods can only expand in the future. The defining lines between forwarder and integrator airlines and handlers are becoming more blurred. The example of DHL, which has gone from being a simple integrator to performing an entire range of cargo and postal services, has set new dimensions in this sector. Even FedEx is involved in ocean freight. This points to this sector of aviation logistics certainly developing very quickly in the coming years.

Special air cargoes

10

Sometimes using air freight is the only transport solution for a variety of niche cargoes. The reasons for this are varied and often change due to circumstances. Most of this traffic is carried on chartered freighter aircraft suitable for a specific task; charter brokers serving this market are expert in matching aircraft to shipment. The fashion industry is a perfect example of the mix between different modes of transport. High-value collections or latest fashion launches which must be in a particular destination on time will probably employ air freight or integrator, while low-cost mass-produced garments will mostly travel by sea. With a worldwide market for high-cost goods, there is also the extra security that shorter transit times provide.

Orchestras, music groups, art and museum exhibitions, even election equipment, all travel regularly by air and in the case of a world tour, may charter one or more freighter aircraft for the duration of the series. Ground handling of these delicate shipments requires exact timing by highly skilled experts. There is a huge year-round movement of horses for racing, show jumping and breeding. Specialist air charter companies such as ACS, Instoneair and Chapman Freeborn handle this growing trade.

There is an almost constant demand for suppling medicines and life-saving equipment with many operators giving their services free. This is another sector where aircraft play a vital role. Lack of available landing sites is often a drawback and sometimes relief supplies must be dropped over the site. However, some aircraft types such as the AN 12 and C-130 Hercules, adapted from military aircraft, are designed to operate on rougher terrain than standard civil aircraft. In addition, much of the relief supplies are dropped or delivered by military aircraft.

When a disaster occurs, fast response to the emergency is essential and air transportation is often the quickest way to deliver supplies and services to save lives at risk. According to the International Federation of Red Cross and Red Crescent Societies (IFRC), in the immediate aftermath of a disaster these primary aid items include food, water, temporary shelter and medicine.

An effective and coordinated logistics operation becomes crucial in saving lives and diminishing the impact of diseases. The role of the IFRC's Global Logistics Service is to ensure that the IFRC has a robust, competent and efficient logistics capacity to effectively carry out its humanitarian assistance activities and achieve its goals. Its mission is to create a world-class service to support the core work of the Red Cross/Red Crescent network and to share resources with other humanitarian organizations.

Charter brokers

Globalization has transformed the broking industry – in the 1960s and 1970s it was very rare for a broker to contract a series of flights, but in today's world of product launches and hyped products manufacturers of everything, be it the latest cell phone or computer product, need to get their product to market with the minimum of delay. It does not have to be an existing product; it can be a new item like a smokeless cigarette that a manufacturer wants to blast out there. Such launches, although handled by a freight forwarder, very often wind up being chartered through a broker who would know which aircraft were available and reliable.

Animals

Thanks to a number of improvements in animal health technology and relaxation of rules, there is a thriving and profitable market for transporting animals by air. At present this traffic represents no more than 4–5 per cent of airline revenue, which is still significant.

The control of this traffic in live animals requires a wide variety of conditions and international regulations for the animals' health and condition, and for the grooms and attendants accompanying them in transit. The airlines transporting the animals must not only provide the right facilities – stalls, cages and safety levels – but they must also, in their own interests, ensure the integrity and safety of the aircraft. While horses, breeding stock and large zoo animals will usually be transported on board a freighter aircraft, smaller animals such as cats, dogs, monkeys and fish are most likely to travel in the belly-hold compartments of passenger aircraft such as the new generation aircraft with considerable hold cargo capacity. Although restrictions on the global movement of animals have been greatly eased in recent years, airports are governed by strict regulations for quarantine, and phyto-sanitary controls are in place in all countries. It is equally important to guarantee the provision of a calm, humane environment as animals suffer considerable life-threatening stress during travel.

Regulations governing the transport of animals are applied by each national department of agriculture and health, which will vary from country to country, but international rules will also apply. The company shipping the animals will need to ensure that the appropriate documentation and licences are obtained well in advance of the flight. Despite the combined efforts of the global regulatory bodies, many of the regulations are ignored in some countries and the illegal trade continues to flourish. Regulations are set by IATA and the protection of endangered species is governed by CITES (Convention on International Trade in Endangered Species) regulations.

Animal diseases and regulations

IATA publishes its Live Animals Regulations (LAR), which cover all aspects of how to transport animals safely, legally, efficiently and cost-effectively. Many animals are transported for breeding purposes, with the aim of improving conditions and stock quality in developing countries. The regulated companies and organizations involved in this business are dedicated to the humane and safe movement of this precious cargo.

Diseases have had the effect of decreasing the transport of some farm animals as outbreaks occur around the world and strenuous efforts are made to contain and restrict their spread. The main diseases are rabies, foot and mouth disease, bluetongue, bovine spongiform encephalopathy, equine influenza, equine infectious anaemia, equine piroplasmosis, equine rhinopneumoritis, glanders, equine viral arteritis, classical swine fever and avian influenza.

Animals are broadly classified as follows:

- Pets (which may include some laboratory animals).
- Agricultural – cattle, pigs, sheep, goats, poultry.
- Horses and other equine species: this category includes racehorses, show horses, polo ponies and breeding stock.
- Zoo animals, including dolphins, sharks and whales: as most zoo animals cannot tolerate a long journey time, air transport is often the best or only solution.
- Exotics, including monkeys, lemurs, tropical birds, snakes and reptiles, insects and a number of rare breeds: this is a highly

controversial subject as in the past many rare breeds have been smuggled into western countries illegally, often resulting in death of the creatures.

- Semen, eggs, insects.

Pets

Normally airlines consider dogs, cats, ferrets, rabbits and hamsters as pets. However, some companies may also move snakes, turtles, reptiles and amphibians as well as mice, rats, guinea pigs and insects. Most of the traffic, however, is for families taking conventional pets to new locations for work, retirement or vacation. Regulations vary according to the national agricultural and health administration, which sets controls for vaccinations against rabies, etc. In the United States, for example, the Department of Agriculture (USDA) sets the requirements for animal welfare, covering not only air and road transport, but also pet shops and boarding kennels. In the United Kingdom, DEFRA (the Department for Environment, Food and Rural Affairs) does much the same thing. Each country has its own equivalent controlling body, but the rules are very similar.

It is estimated that some 2 million pets are shipped worldwide annually. Some animals will be transported independently of their owners, while many will accompany them on the same aircraft. The busiest markets for pet transport are North America, Australia and Europe, and airport authorities are obliged to provide the necessary inspection and border controls.

Horse transport

Most large animals such as horses are transported in chartered freighters together with their grooms and attendants and may well be delivered to an airport with specialist facilities. In the case of racehorses, for example, they will usually be landed as close as possible to the racecourse to avoid extra-long and stressful road links.

Due to the increasing costs of air transport, only those animals of high value are likely to warrant air transfer. Such value can be commercial, as with racehorses and equine competition horses moving to show events. There are also horses moving between champion breeders, or the flight can be part of a programme to preserve rare breeds. Although the traffic is less than it was a few years ago, it is estimated that some 20–25,000 horses are flown every year.

The journey recovery time for a horse will vary considerably depending on the length of the flight. For example, horses would fly into England from Ireland and race the same day then fly back. From Turkey or the Middle East, the horse would fly on Wednesday for a Saturday race. To and from further afield it would require at least a week and in the case of Japan, 10 days are needed, while Australia has two-week arrival quarantine, so a much longer period of rest is required.

On the ground, horses require very special attention to avoid stress and panic. For events such as the Olympic Games, when up to 200 competing horses are handled within two to three days, enormous skill and planning are needed, but overall very few problems have occurred during the many years of successful horse transport.

Zoos and exotic creatures

The traditional role of zoos has evolved to provide refuge for threatened or rescued wildlife, as centres for education, conservation, biodiversity and the preservation of endangered species. Loss of natural habitat, changing weather conditions, especially drought, plus tribal war and poaching, have seriously threatened the world's wildlife. The safe transport of these animals is a vital part of preservation efforts. Some animals might be moved for better breeding conditions or a particular zoo could be facing closure.

WAZA – the World Association of Zoos and Aquariums – provides guidance, support and help for zoos and organizations involved in animal care, welfare, conservation of biodiversity, environmental education and global sustainability.

Airport animal centres

In controlling the movement of animals, including pets, the primary task is to enforce animal health regulations that apply to pets, livestock, horses, fish, reptiles, invertebrates, coral, as well as eggs, pupae and animal products. It is now possible to move pets anywhere in the world provided the documentation and vaccination requirements are met. These control centre posts are in place at most major airports. Such centres may be run by airports themselves or in some cases by airlines.

Following the 9/11 terrorist attacks in September 2001, airport security has been greatly intensified, which in turn has eliminated most of the smuggling of small animals by airline passengers. The biggest single challenge now faced by the reception staff is incorrect documentation, which can lead to the confiscation or incarceration of the animal until the papers are correct.

Cattle and farm animals

Today, farm animals are flown around the world mostly as breeding stock required by countries wishing to improve domestic quality. In China, for example, now that the population has acquired the taste for meat on a regular basis, significant numbers of beef cattle are being imported to increase local herds. Pigs and more exotic animals such as buffalo are being bred for the table. The majority of shipments are carried out by chartered freighter aircraft.

Lift off for heavyweight freighters

An important sector of air logistics is transporting very large or heavy pieces of cargo, which very often cannot be sent on public roads. This may be for security or sheer size or weight. The kind of item termed 'outsize or heavy lift' could be a piece of oil drilling equipment, a rail locomotive or even an elephant. These shipments are handled by specialist charter brokers and carriers that operate the appropriate aircraft for the job.

The world's air cargo fleet in 2012 was smaller than it was in 2003, but if that vital load absolutely must be there on time, moving a single-piece heavy lift cargo of over 180 tonnes in weight by air is quite possible, writes Ian Martin Jones, editor of *Heavy Lift & Project Forwarding International* magazine.

The list of aircraft capable of handling really heavy cargo is very short. In terms of a flying machine that can scoop up a 100-tonne single-piece load and safely lift it into the air, there is only one commercially available option in the marketplace – the AN-124-100 freighter.

Many may tell you that there are a few other 'one-off' options still flying, but in terms of everyday commercial reality – a commodity that the freight forwarder understands only too well – the AN-124 freighter is the only choice.

The large commercially produced assembly line aircraft like the B747-8F, the B747-400ERF, B777F, A330F and MD-11F have a large payload capacity – up to 140 tonnes in the case of the B747-8F – but the single-piece weight is restricted because of reinforced floor strengths and upwards of single-piece cargoes weighing more than 21 tonnes their use as heavy cargo carriers is restricted.

There is notably one version of the Antonov AN-225 in the air capable of lifting up to 250 tonnes of cargo. It is a stretched version of the AN-124 freighter – and as the world's largest air cargo lifter it constantly grabs the media headlines – but there is only one version of this aircraft flying and, much like the AN-124 itself, rumours that further similar behemoths will one day come rolling off the assembly line again are fairly sketchy in the foreseeable future.

The AN-225 was originally thought up by Ukraine's Antonov Design Bureau in support of the Soviet space programme to airlift the Buran space shuttle and its rocket's boosters. The single version flying is operated by Antonov Airlines, and is commercially available for carrying ultra-heavy and oversize freight up to 250 tonnes. It can accommodate single pieces up to 210 tonnes.

In August 2009 the heaviest single item ever sent via air freight was loaded onto the AN-225. The consignment was a generator for a gas power plant in Armenia and its loading frame weighed in at a world record 187.6 tonnes.

Battle proven

In the days of the Cold War, the AN-124 itself was developed initially to lift battle tanks and support troops into frontline combat zones, and it is still the world's largest military aircraft currently in service.

A total of 56 AN-124s were built in parallel at the Antonov complex in Kiev, Ukraine and at the Aviastar-SP factory in Ulyanovsk, Russia and most of the fleet still remains in the hands of the military and, despite much speculation, these are unlikely ever to be released into commercial service.

Production of the AN-124 halted after the break-up of the Soviet Union; however, the first of three new airframes was delivered to Volga-Dnepr Airlines in 2000 by Aviastar. The airframes incorporated new design changes which increased the service life of the plane from 7,500 hours to 24,000 flight hours.

Other planes were derived from the AN-124 and used for commercial service. These include the higher payload AN-124-100M and AN-100-150 versions, and the next-generation AN-124-300.

The AN-124's maximum payload is 120 tonnes over a range of 4,650 km, although much heavier loads have been carried over short distances. The size and density of the load will determine the weight and range, but this versatile machine is in general use around the world for hundreds of varied purposes, including yachts, locomotives, pop groups and even the infamous EP-3E Aries II electronic intelligence aircraft from Hainan Island, China.

Lighter heavy cargo

For lighter loads of around 50 tonnes there are modernized versions of the Ilyushin IL-76 and a few old 'rust bucket' aircraft like the AN-12 and AN-26 freighters that can still offer lift into regions where the environmental issues come well down the list of priorities.

The modernized IL-76TD-90VD is a ramp loading heavy cargo aircraft with a 50-tonne payload capable of autonomous loading without the use of special airport equipment. This opens up the possibility of using the aircraft at airports with an undeveloped infrastructure.

Like the AN-124, the IL-76TD-90VD has a tail loading entrance with expanding loading ramps. The cabin is also equipped with two electric winches of 3 tonnes traction each and four electric hoists with a pulling capacity up to 10 tonnes. Russia's Volga-Dnepr Airlines operates the upgraded IL-76TD-90VD aircraft that meet the European and US noise and emission standards.

The Lockheed L-100 Hercules produced the civilian version of the C-130 military transport aircraft until 1992 with 114 having been delivered but, in February 2014 Lockheed Martin relaunched the LM-100J as replacement for the existing civilian L-100 fleets.

Oversized cargo

The list of commercial freighter aircraft able to accommodate oversized cargo is slightly longer, but payloads are limited, particularly in terms of dense single-piece cargoes that would simply drop straight through the non-strengthened floors of most commercially built freighters.

With US aircraft manufacturer Boeing holding a 90 per cent share of the heavy air freighter market, it is here that the nose-loading capability of the production built B747-400 and B747-8 freighters come into their own, enabling extra-long cargo to be loaded straight into the full length of the aircraft's cargo compartment.

Able to fly 8,130 km with a full load of cargo, the B747-8F achieves a 16 per cent lower operating cost than the B747-400F, while offering a slightly greater range. With a 30,177 cu ft (855 cu m) main-deck cargo compartment it is often used to move machinery or indivisible loads that require a higher payload and landing capability from the carrying aircraft.

The Boeing B747 Dreamlifter is an extensively modified Boeing 747-400, produced in Taiwan and used exclusively for transporting Boeing 787 aircraft parts from suppliers to assembly plants around the world. The cargo hold of the aircraft is 65,000 cu ft (1,840 cu m) and can accommodate three times the volume of a standard B747-400F freighter.

A fleet of converted Airbus A300-600ST (Super Transporter) Beluga freighters are maintained by Airbus and, as well as oversized cargo, are used to carry prefabricated aircraft parts from worldwide production centres to the Airbus assembly line in Toulouse, France.

Both Airbus and Boeing utilize their Beluga and Dreamlifter fleets to carry aircraft parts; however, the Beluga fleet also contains specially heated and pressurized cargo compartments. This has meant the Beluga has been used on occasion to transport space satellites, fine art paintings and other such large and delicate cargo. In 1999 Delacroix's 'Liberty Leading the People' was transported from Paris to Tokyo by a Beluga when it was realized that the huge canvas – 2.99 m (9.81 ft) by 3.62 m (11.88 ft) – was unable to fit into a Boeing 747. The aircraft's maximum payload of 47 tons makes it of very limited use for 'heavy-lift' items.

Recent problems faced by the road haulage industry, such as the strike of French workers at Calais together with the increasing numbers of migrants, brought the heavy lift aircraft operators into unexpected action. A large amount of urgent cargo, caught up in this blockage, was subsequently flown across the Channel, albeit at a high price. These operators are always on the alert for such opportunities.

Flying fashion

The textile and clothing industry is a completely globalized business, using all modes of transport. The high end of the fashion trade tends to use air freight mostly due to the high value of the goods and very limited shelf life. Global design and sales of clothing and high fashion have become a multi-billion dollar industry, employing millions of people around the world. The demand of the fashion industry for ever-changing styles means the producers are under great pressure to fulfil customers' needs. At the high fashion end there is a need for quick delivery with high levels of security and safe conditions. Market characteristics constantly change from country to country. In addition many shipments are of very high value and sensitive to temperature and rough handling, so greater care is needed to ensure that the goods arrive in perfect condition.

Some manufacturers, such as Zara, are developing online business to avoid the high overheads of retail outlets. Air freight is very often the shippers' choice but not in every instance, as more shippers turn to sea freight. At the mass-produced end of the spectrum, large quantities of garments are transported in containers by ocean freight. Almost 30 per cent of all garments produced in the world are exported from developing nations. Hence, there is a large cost involved in transporting materials and finished goods.

The UK example

Until about two decades ago most buyers placed their orders on a 'delivered' basis, which meant that the seller was responsible for arranging transport and – unless alternatives had been agreed during negotiation – typically would use the cheapest option available, which meant that supply chains were opaque, with limited information and often no warning of impending deliveries. By the mid-1990s extended international supply chains were maturing and importers were starting to see the benefits of changing their buying terms so that they could take control of their own supply chains.

Traditionally air freight was the mode of last resort for shippers. At up to 30 times the price of its sea freight alternative, it was an expensive choice that was made because:

- Demand justified getting product to market quickly.
- High product values offset the cost.
- Luxury goods may benefit from the additional security.
- The factory messed up. They can pay for air freight.

While the cost of air and sea are at opposite ends of the scale, so too are their transit times. Sea shipments originating in the Far East and Indian subcontinent could take up to 45 days from leaving the factory to arrival at a UK warehouse, while premium air freight services could achieve the same in as little as 72 hours.

In the late 1990s, fashion brands and clothing retailers, with their acute sense of emerging trends, saw that they could use this transit time imbalance in their favour, selling popular lines without competition for maybe a whole season. One of the leading high street names went so far as to turn supply chain strategy on its head by selecting air freight as its primary transport mode across all lines. It then concentrated on speeding up every supply chain process from range planning and design, through production, despatch and shipping. The objective was to create the most efficient and responsive supply chain that could react to, and satisfy, emerging demand within a matter of weeks. Forwarders reacted to these changes by developing a series of added-value services, in effect adapting their operations for handling and processing garments, thus streamlining the supply chain even further.

With import supply chains becoming increasingly effective, the demand for greater flexibility grew. Shippers wanted more choice than simply 'premium' or 'deferred' air freight at one end and slow sea freight at the other. The challenge was for forwarders to develop alternative shipment choices from all the major sourcing origins, to offer shippers a choice of transit time and cost, so they could match more effectively with demand.

From Shanghai, for example, shippers had six modal options, which could in turn be finessed even further:

- premium air – 1 day;
- deferred air – 3 days;
- air–road – 6 days;
- sea–air – 15 days;
- rail–air – 9 days;
- sea – 35 days.

The advent of so many modal opportunities globally has led to an unintended decline in service quality for many shippers, in particular the use of third-tier carriers and unsuitable trans-shipment points for modal changes. In an effort to address this the latest air freight developments are in the use of premium shipping lines, 'flag' air lines and ultra-secure trans-shipment points, at low-demand points, to provide the best possible service at extremely competitive rates.

Art craft

Every time you go to a big concert or art exhibition, the chances are that what you see has been flown in from around the world. Artists such as Madonna or the Berlin Philharmonic Orchestra will require at least one or even two dedicated wide-bodied freighter air craft to move their equipment from venue to venue. It is highly specialized and skilful work and depends on careful timing and planning.

Jean-Claude Raynaud of Air France-KLM-Martinair talks about the specialist movement of fine art:

Air France Cargo as well as KLM Cargo regularly carry various 'Art commodities', paintings and museum pieces, the main article being primarily famous and valuable paintings which regularly travel from one museum to another and back to the original museum a few months later (for instance from the Musée du Louvre or the Musée d'Orsay in Paris to the Metropolitan

Museum or the Guggenheim Museum in New York). This is also true for private paintings belonging to private galleries or owners (private collections). This is routine business for the airline. Of course considering the high value of these paintings, high insurance cover is compulsory during their entire transit from museum to museum and back.

A specialist from the museum always accompanies these precious shipments from the departing museum to the arriving museum, and they fly on board the same aircraft as the art objects, whether it is a passenger aircraft or a full freighter. So the control is permanent. As for all fragile and valuable commodities, they require special attention and a special type of packaging, which is done at the museum by specialists under the permanent control of the museum. Of course this applies at both ends.

Here again, and as for all freight, the role of freight agents is particularly essential and those who specialize in 'art' are a few dedicated ones who generally only handle this type of cargo. For instance in France we have specialized freight agents such as: LP Art/André Chenue/Crown Fine Arts/Air Cargo Marketing, just to cite the main ones. The main destinations, and you will probably not be really surprised are: United States (New York/Los Angeles/Chicago/San Francisco), Japan (Tokyo), Mexico and Beijing.

In terms of weight this is very little compared to the thousands of tons we carry on a yearly basis, but in terms of value carried it is more significant quite obviously. And in terms of turnover, compared to the total/global turnover of all freight we carry per year the figure is quite small. But what is more important is the fact that if those specific customers choose your airline as an 'art' carrier it is for your 'know how' and your reputation for quality and reliability, and to that extent, it is important for a carrier to belong to this little group of 'happy few' airlines chosen by these customers to do this delicate and sensitive transport.

On the grid

Motor sport has become one of the world's most popular activities involving huge amounts of money. Whether it is F1 world championship or rallying cars, air transport is frequently the solution of choice or necessity.

Transporting F1 equipment

Along with a wide variety of automotive competitions that take place around the world, the Formula 1 race calendar challenges its organizers throughout the season. With events taking place in countries continents apart, cars, equipment, spare parts and technical teams must be packed, flown and unpacked ready to roll to precise schedules. Each race team travels

FIGURE 10.1   F1 car loading by DHL

around 160,000 km per season for races and test sessions. While it is clearly more economical where possible to move the equipment by road, many of the events involve long intercontinental routes. As a logistics operation it is extremely complex and time-sensitive. DHL is the chosen official logistics partner for the F1 World Championship managed by Formula One Management (FOM). Apart from the considerable task of organizing hotels, travel, local facilities and communications, when the events are 'flyaway', specially equipped freighter aircraft are used.

DHL handles the flights only, which often will move from one race venue to another without returning to base, which entails loading and carrying reserve equipment.

Conclusions

Overall, loads from a few kilos up to 150 tonnes are routinely flown around the world, some in chartered freighters and increasingly in the bellies of the new wide-bodied aircraft that have been flooding the market. Exotic animals, race cars, locomotives, fashion collections, gold bullion, diamonds, personal effects, vaccines and human body parts are just a few of these special cargoes regularly moved by air. The equipment and logistics technology may change but the trade continues. This shows the diversity of the air logistics business.

Cargo security and risk

11

As a consequence of the high value of the products moved by air, making shipments and planning secure is a major undertaking for logistics operators. There are so many different types of risk or threat that require constant attention. Some can be defended against by the use of careful planning and monitoring, but others are more difficult. Logistics operators themselves can unknowingly create extra risk by keeping to minimal inventory only to find that some event beyond their control has stripped their supplies bare. Criminal gangs are also working hard around the world to separate high-value freight from its owners. This chapter provides a brief review of the main security dangers that lurk in the shadows and that can ruin a profitable transaction. The main risks include:

- crime, on the increase;
- terrorism, constant threat;
- natural disasters and weather, constant threat;
- health hazards, unpredictable;
- cybercrime, on the increase;
- corruption, permanent problem.

Crime

Criminal gangs have recognized for years that air freight shipments are valuable and are thus highly attractive targets which, due to the fragmented transport chain, are comparatively easy to access. This is always when the freight is on the ground. While cargo is in the air the only risk is of a crash but the minute the wheels touch down, the danger starts.

Considering that one container of mobile telephones could be worth several million dollars, it is well worthwhile for the criminals to attack it. If the movement of this item has been identified and signalled in advance to the outside criminal, stealing the item becomes much easier. Shipments by air will always start and end their transit in a vehicle or a warehouse where they are most vulnerable.

For several decades, high-value consignments have been easily targeted by criminals and in most cases their task has been made easy by lax security and inside help or tip-offs, plus in many cases reluctance on the part of the victims to report the theft. In the early days, the target was mostly gold bullion, cash and valuables, but nowadays many other cargoes are equally valuable and easy to sell into the black market. High-value robberies over the years have cost and continue to cost the industry and insurance companies billions.

The benchmark incident occurred at London Heathrow in 1983 when a consignment of gold bullion plus around £3 million in cash was stolen quite easily by a gang following an inside tip-off. The gold was never recovered. It showed up the total inadequacy of the existing security.

In 2005 at Schiphol airport in the Netherlands, robbers disguised as KLM airline employees in stolen uniforms drove a stolen KLM truck that had just delivered uncut diamonds due to be taken to Antwerp. With no hindrance they drove away with US$118 million, the largest diamond heist in history. A similar robbery had occurred six months earlier.

In 2013, a package of diamonds with an estimated value of US$50 million was snatched directly off an aircraft on the runway at Brussels airport. Diamonds may be a girl's best friend but they are almost impossible to identify, making them the perfect material for theft.

All these cases shared some common factors. Shipment information was transmitted by employees to criminal gangs. Security was of a low level and swift escape was easy. Since those days there have been many high-value robberies of diamonds, cash, computers, mobile phones, pharmaceuticals and fashion goods.

Cargo theft is of course not a victimless crime because apart from the high risk of injury or death to the personnel involved, it affects everyone in the chain. There is a flow of dirty money from crime into drugs and other illegal activities. Customs duties are lost. Companies which are targeted never really recover the lost business. The United States alone loses several billion dollars' worth of goods every year and the situation in Europe is becoming worse.

Furthermore, US law did not identify cargo theft as a specific crime until the US Patriot Improvement and Re-Authorization Act (2005), when the FBI and other law enforcement agencies realized the extent of the impact of cargo crime on the economy. In the United States and Europe there are often crime syndicates involved, which find unlimited markets for the stolen goods throughout the world. The disastrous 2008 recession created an unprecedented demand for cheaper black market goods that are sold freely through open markets, car boot sales but increasingly via internet sites.

Road theft

It is during the road transit phase of the supply chain that the maximum opportunities for hijacking and theft occur. This is due to a number of factors, depending on the country. Cost cutting may impact severely on the security of the transit. To get a low transport price, short cuts will be taken. A single driver on a long journey will need to stop possibly several times and the vehicle will be unattended. A driver is also limited to the number of hours he or she is allowed to drive and, if there is no guarded truck park available or it is cheaper, he or she may stay overnight in a layby. Also, if the journey is badly planned, the truck might arrive at its destination too late to gain entry to secure parking. In these instances the vehicle is vulnerable to theft – possibly the entire truck itself or its load. Robbers often disguised as police officers add further to the problem as drivers may be signalled to pull over and cannot know whether or not the police are genuine. The driver is often threatened with violence or may show no resistance. If this theft occurs on or next to a motorway, easy escape is at hand.

Drivers who may not speak the language of the country where they are delivering may be given incorrect delivery information and hand the goods over to a hijack gang. Phoney trucking companies may win the contract to deliver the goods and then steal the entire load. Outsourced contractors must be carefully checked every time. If the price is too low, it could represent a potential risk. There have been several instances where a van, with uniformed driver and correct documents, has presented itself at an airport warehouse and departed with a very valuable consignment. The use of tracker devices and bar codes has greatly diminished the risk, but the thefts continue.

Internal theft

The large numbers of staff needed to operate a busy cargo operation mean that there is a constant risk of employing people with criminal backgrounds. Despite careful checks of applicants, it is not difficult for forged documents and references to be presented and the person duly employed in potentially sensitive areas. Staff in warehouses often receive low wages and if such a person sees an opportunity to steal there is very little to stop them. The same problem exists with baggage handlers at airports.

It is possible that the same employees may give out sensitive information to criminal associates. In one example a few years ago at the Paris CDG airside warehouse of one handling company, a gang of heavily armed robbers arrived and took away a newly arrived container of telecom equipment worth over US$2 million. They had received an inside staff tip-off and nobody was prepared to risk their life to resist. The whole robbery was over in a few minutes.

Countermeasures

The answer to fighting these crimes is never simple but the logistics operators can only work effectively and profitably if these weaknesses and holes can be plugged. Control of the process must involve close monitoring of the goods at all times. Today each box can be fitted with barcoded labels, which allow permanent supervision. The e-freight initiative from IATA, when applied, helps considerably to enforce the necessary supervision, and various organizations have been established to help combat theft and protect shipments.

Counterfeiting

Although it is not pure theft in the normal sense, counterfeiting has become a huge international crime problem. An estimated US$250 billion per year of worldwide counterfeit trading is being carried out. It deprives manufacturers, fashion houses, high-tech manufacturers and pharmaceutical companies of legitimate sales and return on investment but also can be dangerous or even lethal for the end user or customer. Phoney pharmaceuticals, fashion goods, shoes, cosmetics and toys, for example, can threaten peoples' health and severely damage the financial performance of the genuine manufacturers. The control of this crime is largely in the hands of Customs in different countries alongside the control of banned goods such as ivory and rhino horns. (To find out more about the WCO visit **www.wcoomd.org**.)

Terrorism

The 9/11 attacks in the United States suddenly focused the world's attention on the whole aviation security issue. Hurriedly formulated new rules and regulations were introduced globally in an attempt to combat future threats.

Furthermore, the failure of different agencies to communicate and share information played a large part in the problem. Although the terrorist nightmare was aimed at ordinary people and governments, the air cargo sector was also swept up in these measures. Easy access to airside airport areas, warehouses and even aircraft, as was once the norm, was open to all kinds of unauthorized people with minimal security clearance. In the current era, however, access has become severely restricted. All staff are now subject to detailed police background checks, making it much more difficult, but not impossible, for a potential terrorist to obtain a job within secure zones.

Although these new conditions have definitely tightened up security in cargo warehouses and handling areas, they were primarily directed at securing aviation against terrorism. However, the strict rules had an additional impact on crime. For example, the smuggling of rare breeds of small animals, drugs and counterfeit goods by passengers, often carried in handbags and carry-on luggage, became almost extinct due to strict X-ray and other examination by Customs. The downside was to make the flying experience into a virtual nightmare.

Although there have been a few well publicized incidents involving cargo flights, passenger aircraft are clearly a more attractive target. One such incident occurred in 2010 when two separate packages containing explosives were discovered, one in London the other in Dubai but both originating in the Yemen and destined for the United States. The placing of the packages, one on a passenger flight Qatar Airways to Dubai, the other on a UPS service to East Midlands, demonstrated that terrorists were capable of penetrating the networks of the two integrators and that in turn meant the entire air cargo sector. Although the industry leaders cautioned against a huge security blanket and the attendant costs and delays, authorities demanded more stringent screening and inspection and the use of explosive detection devices. There were also questions as to why individuals within the integrators' own checking systems had not queried why these items were being sent to the United States. In other words could the process be a pure IT/technical solution or was the human element important? Screening of all cargo loaded onto aircraft is now mandatory worldwide but the search for ever greater security continues.

Sudden terrorist activities pose a constant threat to aviation operations in general and of course cargo is equally affected. For example in June 2014, Taliban militants attacked Karachi's Jinnah International airport resulting in the complete suspension of all flights. People were killed and buildings destroyed, including the main cargo terminal. The airlines operating at this airport suffered considerable disruption, with knock-on effects in the logistics chain. Outbreaks of this kind are more likely in trouble hot spots around the world but as airports offer relatively soft targets where large numbers of people congregate, every airport must take steps to protect itself and its staff against such attacks.

Flight MH17

Traditionally, civilian aircraft overflying national borders were considered safe from conflict. The loss of flight MH17 in July 2014 significantly changed that. The US Federal Aviation Administration, eight weeks prior to the crash, issued a warning to pilots and airlines to exercise extreme caution when the crisis in Ukraine continued to worsen. However, hundreds of civil flights continued to overfly the conflict area without a problem. Events proved that their confidence was sadly misplaced. One of the main reasons for ignoring such conflicts is the belief that the combatants do not possess missiles or aircraft capable of attacking an aircraft at 35,000 feet. A highly sophisticated missile system was, in this case, available to the ground fighters, and such an aircraft would have been clearly identifiable as civilian. The spectre of passenger aircraft being targets for terrorist attacks has heightened the need for aviation security.

The security operators are now applying a multilayered approach to air cargo security, including enhanced screening requirements for known and established shippers, explosive detection canine teams, and covert tests and sudden inspections of cargo operations.

What are the solutions?

More advanced technical solutions and electronic monitoring of shipments are improving security, with tracking systems playing an important role. Fitting more effective locks and vetting all personnel, plus the close investigation of outside contractors, all help the improvement of security. However, the invasion during the summer of 2015 of HGVs by desperate migrants at Calais has underlined the weaknesses in individual vehicles and the vulnerability of the drivers to threats of violence.

The Transported Asset Protection Association (TAPA) is a forum that unites manufacturers, logistics companies, carriers and law enforcement agencies in a common aim to reduce theft and subsequent losses from the international logistics industry. TAPA sets out to identify the problem areas and develop solutions. With thefts increasing every year, companies that apply the TAPA standards are reporting significant reductions in losses.

The biggest risk is always when the high-value cargo is at a standstill at airports, in warehouses or truck stops, and there are a number of other alliances and groups which airlines, handlers and forwarders can join whose aim is to share information and to research better ways of combating crime. These include Cargo Security Alliance, Freight Watch, Security Cargo Network and many more. Insurance companies, which have paid for much of the losses, are working in collaboration with these groups. IATA is the most important organization involved in airline security. It defines the sector and outlines its methods and actions. (See website: **www.iata.org**.)

Why cargo is a target

As security standards throughout the industry have improved, the potential attacker has been forced to seek different methods. Improved passenger and hand-baggage security led to attacks through hold baggage; but as security improves here, cargo becomes a more attractive target, especially as an estimated 80 per cent of cargo is now being carried on passenger aircraft. There is a low personal risk to the terrorist, as most cargo facilities are on industrial estates well away from the airport, and knowledge about how the industry operates is becoming more widespread, enabling people to penetrate the system.

As the International Air Transport System continues to develop and more airports are increasing their capacity, the volume of air cargo is increasing proportionately. Each consignment has a destination air waybill detailing the flight number, so it is now possible to target specific flights. Consignments of air cargo become more likely to be targeted by an attacker as there is a new security regime for in-flight catering in place and measures are being developed for goods going airside, reducing the options for smuggling prohibited items into the security restricted area, and subsequently onto aircraft. Ultimately security is dependent on all persons doing their jobs properly, and is vulnerable to *complacency*.

Note: at the time of publishing, the world is experiencing a new outbreak of terrorist activities, which will impact on aviation security. An EU prompt to find a combined solution is being discussed.

Natural disasters

We have a history of floods, earthquakes, tsunamis, volcanic eruptions, tornados, hurricanes, blizzards, heatwaves, forest fires, mudslides and freeze-ups. Although such events have been recorded for centuries, it is today in our densely populated world with its transport and supply chains that the effects of nature cause maximum damage. There are many who blame these disasters on climate change; what is certain is that our overloading of our land, air and sea resources with concentrated population centres with high-density housing, huge industrial complexes churning out smoke and fumes, all contribute to the damage to the ecosystems, loss of habitat and loss of life. When severe weather or volcanic activity is superimposed on our fragile environment, trouble is never far away. It would be impossible within this chapter to give details of the hundreds of major incidents recorded but we have given a few examples which illustrate the problem.

The United States is particularly subject to violent weather, especially hurricanes and tornados. As there is a well-recognized season and pattern for hurricane activity, the arrival of a major storm is largely predictable. Although the warning system works well, the power and direction of these storms are not easy to anticipate. Tornados are even more unpredictable. Historical records show major lethal storms and earthquakes dating from all centuries since biblical times and in most cases they have resulted in thousands of dead.

For example, *Hurricane Katrina, New Orleans, 2005* caused 1,326 deaths and left nearly 300,000 people homeless. Reaction by the authorities was incredibly slow and ineffectual: the Federal Emergency Management Agency (FEMA), which was responsible for transporting vital humanitarian supplies, was just not prepared for the problem, even though violent hurricanes occur every year. The resulting chaos demonstrated the vulnerability of the high-pressure US transport and logistics infrastructure. A further four major hurricanes have hit the United States since Katrina. Subsequent snow storms and East coast floods have paralysed the US economy on several occasions, albeit briefly.

The *Eyjafjallajokull* volcano eruption in Iceland in 2010 took the world's aviation industry completely by surprise by blasting the skies with volcanic dust and grit, forcing many airlines to ground their fleets due to the supposed destructive effect of dust on jet engines. The impact on air travel and cargo shipments was immediate and it took several weeks for the problem to evaporate. Airspace was shut down in the United Kingdom, Scandinavia, Austria, Germany, Benelux, Latvia, Poland and elsewhere. Shippers caught up in this ban tried hard to find alternative transport such as road and sea but the volumes involved were too high for the capacity. Perishables arriving into Europe were diverted to southern airports such as Athens and Istanbul, which were unaffected, which necessitated a long road journey to northern destinations. All this caused loss of business and changed the perception of the integrity of air cargo for many shippers. With better planning, superior packaging and sophisticated containers, more and more goods can now be transported cheaply by road, rail and sea.

Sichuan, China, 12 May 2008. The Sichuan earthquake was a deadly earthquake that measured at 8.0 magnitude. The quake killed about 70,000 people and left more than 18,000 missing. Estimates put direct damage and losses from the earthquake at US$29 billion, with collateral damage much higher.

The Japanese tsunami of 2011. Up to 20,000 people were either killed or have gone missing as a result of the horrific tidal wave that left nothing standing. The aftermath of the 11 March earthquake and tsunami, including the crisis with the Fukushima nuclear power station in Japan, has been devastating. According to the World Bank, losses of US$23–300 billion have been estimated. The devastation hit the country's electronics and automobile components manufacturers badly and caused problems for factories in other countries starved of products and parts. By outsourcing manufacturing, some production was saved but it revealed weaknesses in the supply chain. How could any company plan for a disaster of such magnitude?

Haiti has suffered many disastrous earthquakes and storms for several centuries but it is the one of 12 January 2010, magnitude 7.0, which is probably best remembered. The earthquake killed between 46,000 and 316,000 people. Its epicentre was approximately 25 km from Port-au-Prince, the capital. A dozen secondary shocks of magnitudes ranging from 5.0 to 5.9 were registered during the hours that followed. A second earthquake of magnitude 6.1 occurred on 20 January 2010 at 06:03 local time. Its epicentre was approximately 59 km west of Port-au-Prince, and at least 10 km beneath the surface. In this instance, huge international efforts were made by the logistics community to deliver aid, medicines and food.

Governments and communities are always at the heart of the efforts to recover from such events, Manufacturers and logistics companies have learnt many hard lessons in contingency planning and adapting to violently changed marketing conditions. It is clearly a vital part of logistics management to look at every practical solution to such climatic or natural events and make supply chains more adaptable.

Health hazards

Recent history shows that thanks to air travel and international trade, diseases, both human and animal, circulate rapidly. While global responsibility rests with the World Health Organization (WHO), the control of disease lies firmly in the hands of each individual country. Some are efficient, some are not. The spread of SARS (Severe Acute Respiratory Syndrome) or the avian flu epidemic caused massive disruption to daily life and in turn impacted on supply chains.

In the same way as logistics companies and manufacturers are having to make contingency plans in case of natural disasters, the same culture must apply for outbreaks of epidemics. It is simply not possible to anticipate such events, but some kind of strategy must be in place. For example, in August 2014, several airlines decided to suspend flights to Liberia and Sierra Leone as concerns mounted about the spread of the Ebola virus. The WHO also advised people against travel or trade in and out of Guinea, Liberia and Sierra Leone. (To find out more about world health protection, visit the WHO website: **www.who.int**.)

Interview with Doug Brittin, Secretary General of TIACA

Doug Brittin

The security of air freight has become a major global issue. Is the total screening of all air cargo physically possible?

Total screening of all air cargo is a daunting task, and one which is neither attainable nor necessary. The reasons reflect the challenges of the air cargo supply chain itself, the diverse customers it serves, and the diverse models of how they are served. Certainly, it has been proven that '100 per cent' can be attained in limited circumstances. Specifically, the US mandate for 100 per cent screening of cargo on passenger aircraft within, out of and into the US was a legislative requirement that had to be met. Within the US, the ability to allow forwarders and even some shippers to screen cargo was attained at a significant cost, one which was borne by industry itself. But it was also accomplished and enabled by an increase of over 400 per cent in the number of TSA cargo inspectors to ensure compliance. The ability to fund that level of oversight does not exist in too many markets. For inbound US cargo, the mandate was met through the adoption of acceptance of a 'certified' validation that the non-US measures were deemed commensurate (by TSA) with US programmes.

Of course, this only takes into account the cargo transported on passenger aircraft. The overall volume carried on freighters (shipments) far surpasses that which is transported in passenger bellies. Thus, while it might be relatively easy to screen a large shipment through the certified cargo programme (supply chain screening) as is allowed in the US, it would be difficult, if not impossible, to physically screen the millions of small packages transported daily by express carriers. The speed with which they move also makes effective screening difficult. It certainly can be done, but only at the cost of lowering the speed with which such packages move. This is not something which is appealing to consumers, who demand instant gratification in today's 'e-commerce' world. The latter is further complicated by the dramatic increase in packages moving via the postal stream, which still ends up on passenger or freighter aircraft.

However, 100 per cent may not be necessary, and regulators are beginning to take an even more serious look at this. In essence, with the addition of more shipment information, (such as shipper, consignee and other information), tendered earlier in the transport process, regulators can use a risk-analysis format to determine which individual shipments may need a higher level of screening, while others may not need as close of a look. Think in terms of automated passport analysis enabling 'no fly' (or other) measures, or even TSA's 'Pre-check' in the US. The concept behind pre-check is that a great deal of information is known already about the passenger (submitted earlier for vetting), and thus they are subjected to less stringent measures, while other passengers get the full inspection. Ultimately, this should enable the vast majority of passengers to move via pre-check, and the same equation would apply for cargo. The full impact of this is still to be determined, as these advance data regimes (ACAS in the United States, PRECISE in the EU, and PACT in Canada), are still only in the pilot phase. What is certain, however, is that shipment data will need to be more accurate, timelier, and more complete, and the IT programming to connect all of this may well also lead to additional costs for the industry.

Is the industry being priced out of the market by expensive security systems and loss of time?

There is no doubt that the air cargo supply chain has invested millions of dollars into an already high-priced avenue of transport. The infrastructural requirements to support increasing (and evolving) regulatory procedures, as well as the support requirements to physically manage the flow of cargo to satisfy various regulatory bodies, have expanded.

These costs include not only the expensive equipment, but also extensive and ongoing management oversight, as well as significant and ongoing training/retraining of employees. This applies not only to the screening process and equipment, but also toward managing the ever complex security programmes issued by regulators (in some cases several inches thick!).

As an example, in the IT arena, industry must now also worry about providing things such as advance data for regulatory targeting analysis. Additionally, in many cases, we must spend valuable IT time compiling statistical reports for regulators' compliance use. The challenge for industry is that in both cases, much of this still operates the way it did 'back then', using data sets and programs created in IT silos at each company. We must continue to look at how this can be managed more efficiently. Newer concepts such as shared cloud environments may be at least part of the answer, but at whose cost? And in many companies, it is probably still difficult to find IT managers who come out in favour of outsourcing their own jobs. The tendency to 'program it internally' still survives, and as a result, connecting all of these proprietary systems 1:1 to numerous government IT systems adds cost to both sides of the equation. Global regulatory bodies have the same challenge finding common data requirements and channels that might make it easier for industry to operate on a shared platform.

Similarly, the costs and requirements for labour and valuable personnel resources have changed dramatically. To remain vigilant (and compliant) now, companies globally have had to invest in additional personnel to support audit, paperwork and reporting requirements from multiple regulatory bodies – often covering the same types of information but in differing formats. The updated EU ACC3 requirements are but one example of the collateral costs this process entails. Simplifying and standardizing processes would go a long way toward cost reduction in these areas. To remain competitive and viable, industry must continue to explore ways to streamline and reduce these costs. The fact we have done so much already to add mandated security programmes at our own cost, yet remain competitive, speaks well of the flexibility and adaptability of our industry.

Away from the United States and more sophisticated countries where screening is possible, what happens in Third World countries with limited resources? With a new wave of terrorism and political instability, how do operators deal with these counties such as Iraq, Syria and Kenya? Certainly those areas with greater resources are capable of implementing more comprehensive security regimes. What has proven to be effective in areas such as the US and EU is the incorporation of the supply chain participants into the process. But this requires the oversight resources mentioned earlier. In some countries, the government manages the entire screening process, but typically this happens at the airport itself, which is not always the most efficient way to do this, especially with large, pre-consolidated shipments. In others, industry is allowed to screen, with local oversight, but also still at the airport facility.

As we move toward a risk-based analysis of cargo shipments, that may prove challenging in those countries, simply from the ability (or inability) to provide the advance data earlier in the process. Beyond that, programmes such as ACC3 (into Europe), and TSA's inbound security programmes for carriers already dictate what must be done, often in addition to whatever local regulations are in place, and the necessity to then be compliant with both requirements is challenging for industry. As new threat areas emerge, the inbound programmes have a built-in mechanism by which to increase security or screening measures (via emergency amendments and other similar tools), as we saw after the printer cartridge IEDs were shipped from Yemen in October 2010. Typically, however, these inbound security measures only apply from a 'last point of departure' into the regulating country, which can result in cargo being required to be offloaded and screened (even if it was done at origin) at an intermediate transfer point, something we all agree is not efficient either.

Please give your opinion about where you see the next stages of security systems. How helpful is e-freight in this regard and is the aviation industry being held to ransom by political initiatives to introduce unworkable security measures?

The move toward risk-based analysis of each individual shipment seems to be the future. This requires not only a close relationship between Customs and Civil Aviation regulators within countries (and typically these programmes are geared to inbound shipment only), but also with their counterparts in other countries. We can ill afford to have similar types of programmes set up, but then see them created requiring different sets of data, different timing, different risk metrics, and different screening protocols for high-risk shipments. If we can determine a way to properly capture as much 'e' information as possible (such as eCSD), and transmit that information a single time, where the information is viewed by all proper authorities (or based on mutual standards), we can avoid the possible high costs of multiple transmissions of the same information. At the same time, we can avoid possibly having to offload shipments, which can certainly occur if we do not have harmonized procedures. That is why, before any of these advance data regimes become a regulatory requirement, we are pushing for global standards, working closely with ICAO, WCO and the UPU to accomplish this.

Our industry does an excellent job in managing security issues, not just as a requirement, but also to protect their assets, image and, most importantly, their employees (as well as the travelling public). But when an incident occurs, as we have seen in the past, there will always be a public and political hue and cry to do more. That is not likely to change.

Cybercrime

Cybercrime, which is becoming a global menace for everyone, is also part of the air freight security problem. The ability to hack into company systems, identify rich targets, track their location, even forge necessary documents and permits, frequently outwits the experts working on the inside for the operators. The European Cybercrime Centre, part of the EU's police body Europol, has to deal with billions of internet protocol addresses when attempting to trace possible criminal activity. Some intelligence services and large companies are being targeted to steal online data that could lead to trading advantages. Clearly this type of crime will increase in proportion to the logistics industry's efforts to make cargo more secure.

Corruption

Corruption and bribery have been around since medieval times: whenever there was trade there was corruption of some kind. In some countries it has been (and often still is) regarded as legitimate trading practice, a form of necessary tax on business. But with the rise of globalization, the whole corruption problem has become inflated beyond recognition. When a company outsources manufacturing to a Third World country with very low wages, the temptations for officials and local managers to generate illegal or 'facilitation' payments are often irresistible.

The World Economic Forum (WEF) defines corruption as 'the widespread abuse of entrusted power for personal gain'. The term embraces many different types of malpractice including fraud, bribery, pay-offs as well as preferential treatment and in some cases police involvement in allowing illegalities. While strong legislation is well accepted in the United States and most of Europe, in other parts of the world official government agencies may turn a blind eye to it. When wages are low, which is frequently the case in Third World countries with low-level Customs officers or local forwarders, it becomes very easy to obstruct the clearance of a shipment, which can only be removed by bribing the person concerned. Unfortunately there is much evidence of this and even money and humanitarian goods are blocked by local officials or stolen by local militias and politicians. The whole subject of corruption is so widespread and complex that all we are able to cover in *Aviation Logistics* is the basic challenges. To reduce the impact of such practices the most encouraging trend is for companies involved in the supply chain to establish firm links in the chain that are well documented and carried out by reliable and trustworthy contractors.

Conclusions

The entrepreneurs and managers of the air freight industry have tackled adversity and challenges since the first package of mail over 100 years ago. By innovation and tenacity the forwarders, airlines, airports and handlers have developed this business into a multi-billion dollar global enterprise delivering the world's vital supplies and employing millions.

Despite the challenges outlined briefly in this chapter, the business continues to evolve and expand. Very often at the time of human disasters and suffering, it is the air cargo community that steps in with help and equipment. Although there is routine in the daily business, air freight faces endless challenges and opportunities to offer logistics solutions.

The tragic shooting down of MH17 in open airspace sparked heated debate as to where responsibility should lie in declaring flight paths safe. Malaysia Airlines' commercial director, Hugh Dunleavy, vociferously argued that individual airlines should not have to decide whether the skies above war zones are safe or not. IATA and ICAO have made it clear that it should be governments that decide whether airspace is safe or not for commercial transport. However, it is very unlikely that these international bodies will want to take complete responsibility for deciding whether flight paths are safe. Some airlines, through knowledge of danger or reputational risk, will continue to make their own calls on whether they should to fly to certain destinations.

Environment

12

This chapter reviews the impact and political implications of aviation and logistics on the global environment. Aviation is one of the world's most important drivers of economic development, influencing trade, business and tourism. At the same time, despite a successful and expanding sector that creates considerable wealth, jobs and investment, it is the target of environmental pressure to cut down its perceived contribution to greenhouse gases. It is also a highly regulated business sector as well as providing a useful and easy source of extra tax revenues. These factors have created a dilemma of balancing these opposing forces, to which there is no simple solution.

We examine the effect of aviation and its accompanying activities, in the air and on the ground, including emissions, pollution, noise, congestion, nuisance, road traffic and risk. We review current efforts to improve safety and reduce emissions with biofuels, better engine design, route management and aircraft design. We offer informed opinion about the future as well as a hard look at the influence of politics, lobbying groups and business investment.

The issues

During the last decade the powerhouse economies of Asia have created a growing appetite for travel for both tourism and business purposes. At the same time manufacturing in countries such as China, Korea and India has expanded to a dominating position in the global market and in doing so has generated a wealthy new middle class. The hunger for consumer goods and air travel together with the need for air cargo transport has expanded global air traffic to an enormous extent. It was estimated recently that the air cargo trade is worth US$5.3 trillion and has created millions of jobs and is vital to global connectivity. By 2030 the trade is expected to reach some US$6 trillion involving 150 million tons. Despite the significant improvements in aircraft and engine design of an estimated 75 per cent over the last 40 years, aviation is frequently perceived as a heavy polluter of the air we breathe and the air above us and thus a strong contributor to greenhouse gases and global warming.

On the ground, the roar of aircraft over a residential area, and the smoke and congestion from endless lines of heavy trucks are often blamed on aviation activities. Unfortunately cargo also suffers from an additional negative image in that it employs old, noisy and dangerous aircraft that pose extra risks to people on the ground. This impression is totally false today, with a few possible exceptions in some less regulated parts of the world. All aircraft in use internationally carrying either passengers or freight are subject to very strict regulation by international bodies that control and monitor for safety, noise and emissions.

One of the main problems is the high profile of air transport, so that even the smallest incident receives enormous press coverage. In addition there is the perceived danger to the public of air travel and cargo flights. To put this into proportion, approximately 1.24 million fatalities around the world are caused by road accidents each year, which is apparently deemed an acceptable statistic by the national authorities and by the public. The real figure is probably much higher. Unless a mass multi-vehicle accident is involved, most road fatalities go unnoticed and unreported. However, should an incident occur involving an aircraft, such as a crash or even a near miss in the air, the news appears almost instantly in newspapers and TV.

The number of road fatalities per year is distorted by paucity of data from a number of countries with little or no reliable data. By contrast the number of air fatalities is more accurately registered. During 2013 there were 265 deaths from aviation accidents resulting from 16 crashes. The odds of dying in an air crash are estimated at 1 in 29 million, which indicates that travel by air is 62 times safer than by road. The fear of air accidents is irrational and ill-informed. The disastrous disappearance of the Malaysian Airways B777 MH370 (a total of 289 dead), followed by the shooting down of a second aircraft MH 17 (with 298 dead), have inflated the average death rate beyond recognition. Cargo was carried on both flights but this is hardly mentioned. Cargo incidents on freighter aircraft are very rare and in many cases have been caused by incorrectly packed dangerous goods or badly loaded cargo.

Emissions of greenhouse gases are a major challenge for the aviation industry. Combustion generates gases and releases carbon dioxide (CO_2). This is released by aircraft in flight through the burning of jet fuel from turbine aircraft and aviation gas from piston engine aircraft. These emissions are augmented by on-ground vehicles and airport activities. In addition, nitric oxide and nitrogen dioxide which, together, create oxides of nitrogen (NO_x) are released. Water vapour, soot and sulphate particles (particulates), sulphur oxides, carbon monoxide, partly burned hydrocarbons and hydroxyl form the cocktail of emissions released.

The intergovernmental panel on climate change (IPCC) has calculated that aircraft emissions account for around 3.5 per cent of anthropogenic change and could rise to 5 per cent by 2050. Despite continuous research and improvements in engine design and fuel efficiency, these steps forward will be offset by a constant rise in the number of global aircraft movements.

It must be remembered that the substantial investment by aircraft manufacturers in researching, designing and producing a new generation of aircraft is calculated to be amortized over 20 years. Thus rapid introduction of innovations and improvements is not feasible and is rather a long-term project. The Boeing aircraft company regularly reviews its estimates for fleet sizes based on 20-year predictions.

In summary, subsonic aircraft in flight cause the following main effects:

- *Carbon dioxide (CO_2)*: CO_2 emissions are the most common and are considered major contributors to climate change.

- *Oxides of nitrogen (NO_x)*: At high altitudes emissions of NO_x help to form ozone in the upper troposphere. They also reduce methane, resulting in a cooling effect.

- *Water vapour (H_2O)*: This is created by burning jet fuels. At altitude, condensation trails form, comprising frozen ice crystals that deflect a small amount of sunlight away from the surface of the planet and reflect more infrared radiation back towards Earth. This has an overall warming effect on the atmosphere of the planet. A great deal of research has been conducted into the effects of this upon the ozone layer.

The response

The whole aviation sector is the target and while cargo has its own particular challenges, most of the environmental effects apply to both.

The various international bodies are working together to try to establish realistic objectives, with varying success rates. The main organizations – IATA, ATAG, ICAO, FAA – along with national governments need to solve these problems. Improvements could include better traffic control, the avoidance of lengthy stacking of incoming flights at airports, more efficient timetable planning, less waiting on the tarmac for unloading gates or bays, limiting the use of main engines for taxiing and the use of electronic monitoring systems such as XOPS, which by observing all airport units, ensures optimum employment of vehicles. These are just some of the measures that could be introduced comparatively quickly. In some countries, including the

United Kingdom, there are endless disputes about siting new airports or building new runways to improve conditions but these are complex issues often disputed by fiercely opposing camps.

Airports

If a new airport is sited far away from large towns, it cannot function without commercial and residential development. The airport of Paris CDG, for example, was opened in 1974 in the middle of a sparsely populated agricultural region some 25 kilometres north of Paris to remove the congestion from Orly airport. However, over the last 40 years it has grown into one of the biggest and busiest airport hubs and the fifth for cargo in the world, with a large supporting population of workers, transport companies, etc. It has spread its infrastructure in every direction and is home to a vast network of airlines, forwarders, agents, transport companies, offices and residential areas. The airport is living proof of the dynamic and relentless expansion of aviation and its related activities. It is impossible to develop an airport successfully without people, industry, traffic, pollution and noise. Interesting examples such as Hong Kong or South Korea can be seen.

Local produce

Many self-promoting interest groups have gone to extremes in their attacks on air commerce. One example is the threat of a boycott of fresh produce from Africa and flown to the United Kingdom and central Europe. While stopping this trade may have had a very minor effect on CO_2 emissions on these particular routes, many Africans would have been deprived of a livelihood, and fresh produce would have been denied to the public. And everyone knows that freighters will not lie idle if traffic dries up on one route: it will be simply diverted to another, thus doing nothing to decrease global emissions.

There is also a strong belief amongst other groups that these imported crops should be grown locally, thus saving the need for long-haul flights and cutting emissions. While it's clearly attractive for local farmers, the climate in northern Europe and the United States is not favourable for growing many types of crops without the use of large greenhouses, which must be heated at great cost and energy consumption, plus the use of fertilizers (hauled by road) as well as the need to transport to central markets. The combined result is mostly high-priced artificially forced product harvested by slave-wage immigrant workers. In addition, the drive to build housing estates on agricultural land reduces the space available for farming and places a great strain on the land.

In the United Kingdom, the rain-drenched winter of 2013/14 is clear evidence of a problem facing the farming industry, with many crops destroyed by flooding. In other countries such as Germany, the lack of space is a further limitation to agricultural expansion. The southern regions of Europe and the United States produce large quantities of fruit and flowers, which in turn must be sent by road to their markets. The trade in these products is a vital ingredient of the economy and jobs market.

Alternative fuels

Research into non-carbon-based fuel is being conducted with mixed results. Jet aircraft currently operate with a petroleum-based product known as JetA, or JetA-1, but fuels based on synthetics, biofuel, hydrogen, natural gas, ethanol, methanol and propane are possible, although relatively expensive, and not a commercial reality at present.

Biofuel, while being popular with governments wishing to appear socially responsible, is in itself problematic. Vast areas of productive land are necessary to produce sufficient quantities of appropriate vegetation such as soya beans, which is resulting in the loss of forest areas and diverting efforts away from food production to the possible detriment of local populations. However, biofuels mixed with jet fuel have been successfully tested by airlines including, for example, Virgin Atlantic and KLM. In 2011 the Boeing Aircraft Company flew its new B747-8 freighter directly to the Paris Air Show using a mix of 15 per cent biofuel and conventional jet fuel. Other synthetic and natural fuels can be employed, but they are expensive to produce and can burn even more carbons in the process; for instance hydrogen emits large quantities of water vapour and the long-term effects are unknown.

(For more on this topic, see **http://climate-l.iisd.org/news/icao-environmental-committee-agrees-on-new-aircraft-carbon-dioxide-standard/**.)

Political influences

Governments are apt to enthuse about environmental initiatives that make good press coverage and enhance their image. However, the main creators of pollution and environmental emissions such as China, the United States, India and Russia continue to expand their manufacturing and carbon consumption unabated. The emissions caused by industrial activities are far more hazardous to health than any other kind other than nuclear. The creation of millions of tons of exhaust fumes and factory emissions vastly outweigh the part played by civil aviation. Large cities such as Los Angeles or Taipei have endured decades of heavy smog and exhaust fumes. This increasing problem will require a combined international commitment to work out a realistic solution that can be applied effectively.

In February 2014, newspapers reported that the city of Shijiazhuang in northern China was so badly polluted that legal action had been taken against the municipal environment protection bureau to adhere to the law limiting pollution. The European Union became involved in an international dispute by introducing in 2005 the Emissions Trading Scheme (ETS), which was applied to aviation in 2012. The scheme determined that all airlines operating in EU member states should cap their emissions at 95 per cent of historical levels. Those that did not comply would be forced to purchase ETS credits, the funds from which would be retained by the member states. This was immediately seen as a direct tax on aviation and resulted in strong reactions from other non-EU countries such as the United States, China and India, which refused to cooperate. After threats of legal action and an outright refusal to adhere to these unilateral regulations by countries such as the Russian Federation and the United States, the European Commission backed down and a compromise was reached to move the matter to ICAO, and seek a global solution. The ICAO agreement focused on the issues of air and noise pollution, and concluded an acceptable agreement that was free of political and economic arguments, thus defusing the debate between the EU and the rest of the world.

Air freight's extra burden

There is additional public concern about the perceived environmental impact of air freight and the noise its activities can generate, particularly through night-time take-offs and landings, which are vital to make the operators' business models sustainable. Cargo operators favour night-time movements so that they get easier access to slots and carry out overnight hub activities to ensure next-day deliveries. The obsession with 'next-day delivery' depends on these time-sensitive flights. Cologne (CGN) airport, for example, has no night flight ban and is the European hub for UPS and FedEx. Each night it handles dozens of flights, while during the day it is almost entirely passenger flights that form the traffic. TNT, with operations centred on Liège in Belgium, which also has no night-time ban, has benefited enormously from the hub-and-spoke operation.

Many of the airports chosen by integrators such as DHL, with hubs in Leipzig in Germany, Vitoria in Spain and East Midlands in the United Kingdom, have flights operating all night connecting with their main hubs – Paris, Frankfurt, Hong Kong, etc. To avoid and work within night curfews, meticulous planning and scheduling are vital. When Frankfurt airport was instructed to stop night flights, the impact on Lufthansa was severe. Despite this setback, the airline, being one of the world's leading cargo carriers, managed to plan its way forward.

Road Feeder Service (RFS), indispensable for transferring cargo to and from airports, causes huge amounts of heavy truck traffic. Luxembourg-based Cargolux, one of the industry's leading all-cargo airlines, operates nearly all its flights to and from Findel airport in Luxembourg and relies on its cargo in- and outbound to be serviced by trucking services from all over Europe. It is a business model that has successfully allowed it to maintain a fleet of 16 B747-400 and B747-8 freighter aircraft. Despite this, the airport, which has some of the most stringent night curfew rules, still functions – a remarkable achievement for an all-freighter airline.

In Germany, with 23 domestic airports and access to major hubs in the Netherlands and Belgium, the flow of road traffic is increasing at an alarming rate. With the major regional hubs of Frankfurt, Munich and Cologne relying on feeder services from across the country, it is a challenge to reduce this traffic. Within the United States, thanks to cheaper fuel and less long-distance passenger traffic, most goods are transported by road and not by air, at a fraction of the cost. Really urgent shipments are mostly handled by the integrators and courier companies. International flights out of major hubs such as New York, Miami and Los Angeles are serviced by road. As international trade expands, so the potential congestion and emissions increase pro rata. International trade carried out by the logistics industry cannot operate without the vital links of ocean, road and air. All nations are faced with similar challenges.

Innovation and trends in air logistics

13

In an industry as dynamic as transport, survival has always been driven by innovation. From the earliest days of flying, people have sought improvements and increased performance from not only flying machines themselves but the vital ground services without which aircraft cannot function. In recent years the impact of recession, political conflict and terrorism have been some of the major factors in shaping the supply chain and with it, air cargo operations. The global economy is now demanding more speed and efficiency backed by competitive pricing. To achieve this, more technology is being adopted by airlines, airports, forwarders and handlers.

The e-freight project launched by IATA has so far only had a moderate acceptance by the industry, but more operators in the chain are taking on board the need for this. The process aims to remove paper processing from the air cargo transaction, involving everyone – from manufacturer through forwarder, export Customs, handler, airport, airline, receiving handler, airport, import Customs, forwarder and on to consignee. All this must be achieved while reducing costs. In addition to the advances in technology, the development of a new generation of aircraft capable of carrying 25–30 tonnes in their bellies has had a major impact on the price and speed of air freight. (For details of the e-freight system visit **www.iata.org/e-freight**.)

The industry leaders all agree

At the world cargo symposium in Shanghai in March 2015, Leif Rasmussen, President and CEO of SAS Cargo, stated that at present there is a fragmented and bureaucratic value chain from which the industry must free itself. He warned the industry of the example of Kodak, which failed to react fast enough to the advent of digital photography. He further stated that air cargo operators must be willing to embrace radical thinking that would change the way we do business.

Many delegates agreed that to share information throughout the chain more easily would cut inefficiency and increase transparency, allowing the air cargo market to act more like the integrators, which have used this model for many years. According to Robert Mellin, the head of distribution logistics for Ericsson Data, more exchanges between shippers, forwarders and air cargo players could also cut transit times and reduce mistakes but need not cost more.

It was also suggested that data exchange should no longer be based on messaging, but on sharing through a 'cargo cloud', an e-cargo track, to create efficiencies in the supply chain. There were also calls for a more radical transformation of the industry. Oliver Evans, then chairman of TIACA, agreed incremental shifts would not be sufficient, stating that the only thing to do is to totally reinvent the processes, to change the mindset and introduce more radical thinking.

Joost van Doesburg, air freight policy adviser of the European Shippers Council, agreed and wondered if the industry's IT suppliers were sufficiently innovative. He questioned whether the time had come to bring in someone from outside to see it differently and maybe recommend alternative ways of changing the way it should be done. He also opined that the forwarding industry was best placed to lead the change. 'Forwarders need to become integrators without their own aircraft.'

There was general agreement from the 140 or so speakers, and many of the 1,000+ delegates, that not changing was not an option. Mercator's Mr Fernandes said: 'It's time for change, or we'll be left behind. We are all stakeholders in making this happen.'

Awards for innovation

(The following report is published with thanks to *The Loadstar*, the daily global news newsletter for the logistics industry.)

During 2015, IATA scheduled to award up to US$40,000 in prizes for innovation in the air cargo sector. Three nominees were selected for the first of its Air Cargo Innovation Awards. All three from the Netherlands have come up with an idea which not only simplifies certain air cargo processes, but adds visibility to a part of the air freight chain which was previously regarded somewhat murky: CargoClaims by CargoHub, CanTrack by CHEP and Niall van de Wouw's Clive.

First nominee

CargoClaims seeks to simplify the claims process, a notoriously long-winded and frustrating job, known, according to the Dutch company's IATA submission, as 'the headache files'. Launched by CargoHub in January 2014, the system enables all air cargo stakeholders to lodge claims through a single, integrated platform.

'This makes the claims process more efficient and transparent,' said Kiona van de Burg, business development manager, who tested the system with Saudi Cargo. 'Everybody needs to claim – it is part of the business. But it takes time to collect the data, to find the right person. You need to know where it went wrong and what to do. It creates a headache for everybody, and no one wants to claim, but the shipper has to take action. There are a lot of documents, and it's a different process for each airline,' she explained. 'Some airlines already have a claims portal within their core systems, but there has been no centralized system to date where forwarders can manage all their claims.'

Ms van de Burg, who wrote a thesis on claims management, said it was hard to determine the number of claims made, as airlines would be loath to give out those statistics, but that the number was significant. And that claims, in some cases, could take up to two years to be processed. 'It can be worth a lot – airlines can lose key accounts because a customer will walk away over a bad claims process.'

The system collects data on incidents where cargo is lost, damaged or delayed, which could be logged by a handler, as well as claims from forwarders. Given that many claims are submitted locally, but dealt with by head offices, and that both different offices and companies may submit claims in different ways, the platform helps standardize the information. It enables businesses to collect, analyse and exchange data and so will reduce time, cost – and paper.

CargoClaims offers three different user models: Freemium, Premium and Enterprise. The first, free of charge, allows any company to submit a claim to any airline electronically, with all communication and documentation logged and filed. The Premium, a paid-for service, allows for multiple users from one company and provides continuous updates, while the Enterprise model allows for customized service, with integration onto a company's own website, as well as increased visibility into the claim. Customers currently include Saudi Cargo, AviaPartner, MASKargo, Aramex, Panalpina and Kuehne + Nagel.

IATA's criteria for the award were: to be an industry enabler, increasing the competitiveness of air cargo compared with other modes, or enable new commodities to be carried; increase quality and/or decrease cost; and develop technologies that optimize revenue or capacity utilization, or shorten the lead time or enhance service.

CanTrack brings innovation to air cargo with solar power driving valuable data

An innovation from CHEP, CanTrack does what it says: it tracks ULDs. But it does so using solar power; it harvests its own energy, thus overcoming the potential pitfalls of tracking systems which rely on battery life alone.

Working with OnAsset, which already has a tracking device approved for use on an aircraft, CHEP wanted a way to automate tracking its ULSDs – but the downside to existing technology was that it needed to be charged.

'It is completely impractical to run round airports trying to charge units – we have 80,000 of them,' explained Floris Kleijn, CHEP's IT director and project leader. 'So we looked at ways to harvest energy – from temperature differences, or kinetic energy. Those weren't enough to power the batteries of this device. So we turned to a solar panel.'

But is there enough sun during a ULD's average journey?

'As the ULD travels, we see a variation in the ability of the device to charge,' admitted Mr Kleijn. 'We need a couple of hours of sun every two days. If the device reports twice a day it uses 6 to 10 per cent of its power, so it can last for up to two weeks without sun.'

The device is able to record and transmit data on a range of things: impact or shock to the ULD, motion, temperature, light and pressure. Originally designed to benefit CHEP, the team realized it could also provide a wider industry benefit.

'From the perspective of a ULD pooling provider, the first focus was on how to improve asset control,' said Mr Kleijn. 'We developed it with our own interests in mind, but the bigger potential lies in the data which could be shared with all the players, supporting C2K for example. When goods leave your custody, your interest in the data does not end.'

The team identified several points which would benefit the wider industry. By turning the ULD from 'mute' into 'smart' it would: improve ULD stock availability, reduce damage to cargo and ULD by introducing accountability – the ULD would know where damage occurred, improve monitoring of the cargo and its environment, and give real-time information on the whereabouts of the ULD and its contents.

Part of CHEP's submission may not be welcomed by the handling industry, however. An additional benefit of CHEP's submission is the ability to identify where damage happens. 'We believe around 50 per cent of damage is related to the handling of ULDs under the responsibility of GHAs, so by us being able to show where damage occurs, we can work with the GHAs on training programmes to improve handling that will reduce damage, that could save the airlines up to US$50 million a year, so there is significant benefit for all parties.'

Mr Kleijn added: 'Ultimately for ground handlers, the information will deliver value through improved timeliness and accuracy of data. It offers an opportunity to prove that your service delivery stands out versus your competitors. You can use the data to influence behaviour and win or retain business.'

The device is still being trialled with Hawaiian Airlines and Air Canada. CHEP plans to absorb the installation and running cost for the base tracking functionality for existing customers and generate ancillary revenue through charging for added-value services.

The team thinks it ticks the right boxes for IATA's award; they say greater visibility into the supply chain will increase air cargo's competitiveness over other modes; it will increase the quality of air cargo, as well as lower costs through less damage; and it could also improve on-board safety.

'I'm very humbled to be in the company of the other two nominees,' said Kleijn. 'What struck me is how complementary our solution is to the others. They all address different opportunities but they are all about improving the quality of data. The real success of that depends on the ability to turn that data into a benefit.'

Clive claims to 'bring humanized technology to the air cargo domain'

The brainchild of Niall van de Wouw, who teamed with Joe Forbes, of Australia's Biarri group, a commercial mathematics company, Clive's software applications focus on three processes: allocation management, demand forecasting and operations management.

Essentially, it aims to move the industry away from software such as Microsoft Excel – well-used, but described as nothing more than 'an upgraded piece of paper'. Its lack of connectivity and real-time information, as well as time-intensive manual processes, say those in the know, make it an unattractive option for allocation management. The alternative, before Clive, was 'conventional decision support tools, which have high implementation and subscription costs relative to the real benefits they bring'.

However, there is now a third way. 'At Clive, we believe that order and simplicity are the best response to the complexity surrounding commercial decision making in air cargo,' explained managing director Niall van de Wouw. 'So it became our goal to build applications that are just as intuitive to use as consumer apps.' The application for allocation management allows both cargo airlines and forwarders to better manage the request, acceptance, implementation, monitoring and changing of allocations.

Clive already has its first customer, Air Capacity Sales (ACS), a unit of DHL Aviation. Paul Ennis, Managing Director, previously used Excel but stated 'the accuracy of the information was inadequate and there was no real-time visibility on capacity allocation, especially taking into account that DHL Aviation has such a complex network. We have lots of demand for pre-allocated capacity, an amazing leap forward.' He added: 'People feel more empowered to engage with customers as we have a clearer view of what is going on. You never get a second chance to fill an aircraft, and now we can talk facts and figures with customers.'

The second application, to forecast air cargo demand, combines the use of proven forecasting methodologies with the knowledge of the 'crowds' – the market intelligence available in the minds and guts from local staff and partners. A recent Proof of Concept with a global air cargo company proved successful, said Mr van de Wouw, and the application is expected to go live in the next few months. The third application will focus on operations management, which allows cargo companies to act more swiftly, and therefore often more efficiently, on disruptions to flights and shipment planning. The innovation in this application is that the software is based on the principles of artificial intelligence. Once a disruption occurs, different 'agents' representing the interest of individual shipments and flights start negotiating until they find an alternative plan – something which, proven in other transport modes, can be done in a matter of minutes.

Each of Clive's applications supports one direct process, leaving the applications 'clutter-free'. 'We are pushing the technology boundaries to make life easier in this domain,' said Mr van de Wouw.

Changing buying habits

The changes and innovations in progress in the supply chain depend very heavily on technology, but there are other influences at work that are forcing the supply chain operators to rethink their methods. Supplies to industrial manufacturers or perishable distributors continue to demand better and cheaper transport services but the retail business is showing some significant changes. A visit to an average high street in a European or US town reveals an increase in shop closures, endless reduced-price sales and people looking but not buying. Stan Wraight points out below a worldwide trend that explains much of this and how it impacts the air logistics market.

E-commerce and air cargo – where are the airlines going wrong?

Global e-commerce is growing at a rate no one could have predicted, and the effects on traditional air cargo can be devastating if airlines cannot react. Daily we read about high street shops closing, as traditional retailers face up to the fact that their high-cost real estate showrooms are drawing fewer and fewer actual consumers, but more and more 'just looking' clients checking out goods they will eventually order online. 'Bricks and mortar' are just too expensive in this competitive environment. E-commerce is dominated by two entities: the global post offices that look upon this as 'God sent', and integrators which, in their typical entrepreneurial manner, have jumped quickly to place products in the marketplace. But where does that leave scheduled airlines?

The problem is that there is very little that airlines can do unless they take control of the ground operations, and with all the outsourcing that has happened in the past years, that leaves very little room for manoeuvre. The solution seems to be that ground handling companies and airlines are going to have to come together as never before to find a collaborative solution or risk being completely left behind. Put as simply as possible, traditional air freight just cannot compete in a market that is dominated by individual shipments that average just 500 grams in weight. Airlines are locked into an antiquated system negotiated decades ago that looks upon these shipments as either subject to airline minimum charges as dictated by the IATA system, or food for consolidators with all the built-in delays and loss of control that entails.

Is there a better way? I believe there is, but time is running out for the airlines if they want to have any say in how this traffic moves in the future. The key to this is for the airlines to recognize that it's not what happens in the air that will dictate success, it's all about ground handling and their ability to finally sit down and enter into discussions with Ground Handling Companies about something other than price.

US online retail sales are up 15 per cent since 2014, and are expected to hit US\$370 billion by the end of 2017. Europe has overtaken the United Kingdom as the biggest online shoppers in the world with e-commerce becoming a market worth over US\$300 billion by 2017. And everyone knows the story of Asia and the rise of companies such as Alibaba.com. This is an e-commerce platform for small businesses, connecting millions of buyers and suppliers around the world. No matter the size of business, it can find the right manufacturer, exporter or wholesaler to suit sourcing needs – a global community of business-to-business professionals. Amazon, eBay and many others have transformed the distribution business.

Technological advancements and changes in consumer behaviour have created an unprecedented opportunity for these new e-commerce companies. This is especially true with millennials (those born after 1980 is the standard definition), who will make up the majority of online consumers in the coming years. Unlike physical retail stores, e-commerce companies are much more capital-efficient because they don't require brick and mortar stores and have a direct distribution channel to their end customers. Retail high street shops are closing everywhere, and these were the ultimate clients of traditional air cargo. In the air cargo logistics chain, wholesalers, distributors and retailers are most at risk of losing out to factory-controlled e-commerce. And needless to say, these are the traditional clients of the majority of forwarders and scheduled airlines.

Let's look at some of the factors that drive e-commerce companies and consumers to choose a particular mode of transport, and what can happen if traditional players in today's air cargo logistics chain do not change their ways.

Price

Postal mail is certainly the obvious choice for door-to-door delivery when price and ease of use are the leading factors. There are very low minimum charges in postal mail, and large volume shippers can negotiate contract rates that mitigate these minimums. This is particularly important for low-value items that consumers order online.

Integrators have e-commerce solutions for most major manufacturers and also for companies that specialize in e-commerce such as Alibaba and Amazon. Companies such as Apple through Apple.com will ship your next iPhone directly from the manufacturing plant to your door using either FedEx or UPS and, to make it all as simple as possible, shipping is included in the price of the phone.

Time in transit

Postal authorities around the world are seeking creative solutions, and increasing their product offering, as they have seen e-commerce as the replacement for their once very lucrative first class and airmail services. Yet inherent in any system is the fact that they are not in control once the parcels leave their facility.

Integrators have this deficiency of control completely solved and have done so for years with their integrated systems. These give them maximum flexibility in designing a product for e-commerce, but this comes at a cost way above that of the postal authorities in most cases. Customs and shipments either refused or undelivered are an issue. For international shipments this can be a huge problem in consumers' choice of modes, and this is where the integrators have an advantage.

What is the solution for airlines, airports and handling companies?

It is obvious that the rulebook on handling air cargo has to be thrown out in this fast-changing environment if airlines want to become relevant again, or face the consequences of shrinking demand and low prices. This will require a mindset change to the way airlines interact with GHAs, and an understanding that a partnership has to be established that will require long-term agreements based on product development, not just price. Some of the issues that have to be addressed are:

- Yield: if it is done properly it will be far above general cargo rates currently in effect as the client will pay for a much-needed service.

- Speed: much faster than post and could be close to integrator if set up right.

- Safety and security: all cargo screened unlike postal at the moment. All cargo could be shipped compliant with new EU rules that come into effect in 2018. As most e-commerce is not from known shippers, procedures need to be established on the ground.

- Less pilferage than post: fewer claims, fewer complaints.

- Control: back in the airlines' hands, but it must be done in a partnership with GHA, last-mile-delivery partners and must be a true long-term strategic alliance, with commitments by all parties.

- Reverse logistics: returns and non-deliveries, Customs, etc to be taken into account. This is part of the due diligence in establishing the service.

- IT and technology: they exist but investments must be made. This will only happen if all parties in the chain have a true alliance, commitment and security. It will happen, as air cargo will be developed. It's only a question of which airlines, airports and GHA management take the lead. The first to offer such products will be the winners, and air cargo can again become a viable and competitive choice for this new breed of consumers and shippers.

The IATA view

Glyn Hughes, IATA Cargo chief, stated:

> IATA applauds all technology initiatives and multiparty platforms which aim to increase efficiency, add to data connectivity and support industry programmes to increase reliability, transparency and predictability in the supply chain. Technology should be an enabler rather than a blocker, so we also encourage direct connectivity when it is desired by business partners.
>
> Technology providers and platforms have an incredibly important role to play in helping the air cargo industry modernize and innovate and by making technology solutions available to those that require them, increase the ability of more stakeholders to benefit from these efficiencies. However, we equally feel that those who have existing effective and functioning technology solutions should not be forced to use community platforms and incur additional costs, thus a policy of optional usage is desirable.

CASE STUDY   Helicopter delivery – what next?

In New York, London and Los Angeles, DHL Express is employing helicopters for urgent delivery to consignees.

The question is being asked as to whether the era of couriers and messengers has had its day. It seems quite likely, in view of the current drone tests run by integrators and the helicopter delivery service DHL Express offered in major US cities. According to the company, the Chicago flights were launched at the end of April 2015 to provide early morning delivery service for urgent document delivery. DHL Express is the only international express company to employ helicopters on a regular schedule, but in such a highly competitive market, it is sure that others will follow.

DHL International shipments for Chicago enter the United States via the DHL Hub in Cincinnati before transferring to flights to Chicago's O'Hare International Airport. They are then sorted, loaded into the DHL Bell 206B3 Jet Ranger helicopter and transported to the new Vertiport Chicago. Shipments then complete the short final part of the route.

People have been experimenting with air transport for over 2000 years, with Chinese kites, medieval balloons, the 1900 Zeppelin dirigible, through to the era of mechanical flight. The 1980s witnessed the age of the jet, the jumbo jet freighter and today the modern wide-bodied B777 A 340. Each generation of flying machines brings a new dimension to flying both passengers and cargo. Speculation about popular space flights and entering space to achieve rapid global transit is ongoing; the reality is probably not far away.

Views on the future

14

In this chapter we have invited different leaders in air freight to give us their personal opinions about the future of this business. Everybody has a different view but all are agreed that air freight will continue to play a vital role in world trade but the industry must adapt and change to embrace new technologies, ideas and thinking. The future is exciting but always challenging.

Enno Osinga

Senior VP Cargo, Schiphol airport, retired; VP Tiaca, retired

Air freight must reinvent itself in order to continue to play a vital role in international trade. The e-AWB is the first step along a very long road that must end in fully integrated data interchange – so shipments are booked, then monitored and supported electronically at every stage. If air freight remains an obstacle to this process, it will be eliminated.

Airports need to play a more active role in driving efficient and competitive ground handling, which is fundamental to the industry's existence. They must leverage their commercial neutrality to bring together all stakeholders – regulators, government bodies, industry and users – and so facilitate the optimization of processes.

Through organizations like TIACA, the industry has an invaluable opportunity to examine the entire supply chain and understand its own role within it. Air freight is no longer a product, but a component; components that don't work are replaced.

Against this backdrop, Schiphol continues to seek logical processes which best serve the end user, rather than supporting elements of the industry. An illustration of this is the provision of direct airside access for forwarders, which helps preserve the condition of sensitive product.

Alexis Sioris

Q & A Alexis Sioris, Head of Cargo, Athens International Airport

1. Do you think that major international airports take cargo seriously enough? In the case of AIA they clearly do but some such as London Heathrow have been accused of ignoring cargo in pursuit of passenger and retail revenue.

I guess there is no black or white answer to this question. And it might be unfair to compare Heathrow with Athens, the former generating at least 10 times the cargo volumes handled through Athens International Airport. On the other hand, if Heathrow, one of the leading European cargo hubs, cannot set the pace, which airport then? To play fair, there are certainly bigger airports that are cargo-friendly.

To me, what really matters for any airport, be it passenger or cargo driven, is to continuously aim for rapport with its cargo clients. At Athens, our strategy has always been to integrate all members of the local cargo community, ie the airlines, cargo handlers, forwarders and GSAs as well as Customs and the vets and phyto-sanitary officials, under one single roof, the so-called Airport Cargo Community Committee (ACCC). This is the platform where we 'entice' the different stakeholders to respect the rules of the game, coordinate, achieve synergies, and where we give our best to orchestrate new developments. We call this the 'we-approach'. Funnily enough, this spring, 11 years after the conception of the Athens ACCC, Frankfurt, a major cargo hub by all means, came up with its own version of a cargo community platform.

2. The hot phrase at the moment is 'modal shift' which, according to Seabury, is costing air trade over 10 million tonnes over 10 years. Many traditional air freight products, even perishables, are switching to ocean. What in your opinion can the industry do to reverse this trend and how could airports contribute?

Modal shift is a long-term phenomenon and it will most probably continue at a moderate rate for several years to go. This perspective is getting paramount, especially as regards flows from Asia into Europe, considering that Cosco, one of the top three shipping giants globally, is about to move its Europe hub to Piraeus; this would shorten the sea segment of the entire trip from the origin in the Far East to west Europe by approximately five days, as the final transportation leg around Europe to final destination ports such as Rotterdam, Hamburg, Bremerhaven, etc would then be avoided.

The air-transportation cost is definitely the main factor that our industry, including us, airports, will have to address. Along those lines, further perspectives need to be considered as well, such as ways to further increase reliability of services, not excluding downtime due to bottlenecks experienced at major airline hubs. At this point, it is worthwhile saying that competition for additional cargo amongst airports sometimes leads to an unintended modal shift in traffic. A typical example is AIA's endeavour to attract sea–air cargo originating from countries of the East Mediterranean sea: perishable shipments originally foreseen to be flown from Tel Aviv directly to the United States are occasionally shipped to Piraeus sea port and then trucked to AIA to be onwarded from there, instead of Tel Aviv, to the final destination. In this case, cargo is still flown, but the tonne kilometres flown are less.

3. Do you think that our industry should do more to cultivate the general public?

Definitely yes! As the airport's role in the world aviation system has become more and more complex and challenging over the years, airports have evolved and become mature businesses that manage their affairs as commercial entities. Along those lines, they play a central role in economic development, underpinning international trade and investment links, and serving as a catalyst for economic growth and job creation. In addition to the multitude of companies that are related to the aviation industry, there are many businesses that need to be located close to an airport in order to operate efficiently. The latter provide not only more employment and improve a community's economy, but also serve to retain existing businesses and attract new industries to the area.

In the context of the above, Athens Business School and Athens International Airport conducted a study in 2010 that was repeated anew in 2013, whereby it was concluded that Athens International Airport creates more than 63,000 direct, indirect and induced jobs as well as jobs through incremental tourism; this figure corresponding to more than 2 per cent of Greece's GDP.

Evidently our industry (at AIA, further to marketing and PR we have a dedicated department dealing with community matters) should definitely place its utmost endeavour to educate the public regarding such value creation.

4. Give your best guess about what will happen over the next 20 years. Do you think that freighters will survive?

I can see major cargo hubs struggling to increase capacity, also due to environmental concerns. As a result, I would imagine secondary hubs and peripheral airports to win a significant share in tonnage by taking advantage of own merits such as flexibility, ample capacity and eventually a more customer-friendly approach as opposed to bigger and/or already saturated airports. As air traffic will definitely keep rising, I expect to see low-cost carriers entering the cargo business as well. While I think more flexibility as concerns multimodality is in sight, I am more sceptical about the future of freighter aircraft. The ever-increasing route frequency and cargo capacity of wide-body passenger aircraft will drastically limit the need for all-cargo aircraft in the long run. As for the cargo operators, those will definitely survive, mainly away from the world's metropolises and wherever capacity for the transport of perishable and outsized cargo is sought.

Heiner Siegmund

Heiner Siegmund, Managing Director, MediaService Gmb and Publisher of *Cargo Forwarder Global* discusses air freight – a changing industry.

The air freight business is facing notable changes in the coming years, at least in mature markets. In relation to other items, standard cargo volumes will stagnate or see only meagre growth figures with urgent and high-value products like pharmaceuticals, perishables, medicines and life science products increasingly gaining ground. This will lead to comprehensive door-to-door service packages offered by logistics players to shippers and consignees and managed electronically (documentation, Customs clearance, billing, etc), with the air carriers playing an integral part in these tailored supply chains.

The trend in air freight leads towards customization of products and individualized transport solutions. Not only will the pact between freight forwarders/airlines be deepened including handling agents and GSAs, but there will be new business alliances to provide the customers the best service possible. For instance, larger cargo carriers could extend their network indirectly by closely cooperating with passenger airlines that serve beyond-markets but offer only lower-deck capacity. General Sales Agents could become an integral part of this grouping by managing sales in a number of markets the partnering airlines are serving.

Similarly to special products, the segment of oversized, heavy cargo will grow in the coming years. There's always demand for transporting oil drilling equipment, heavy machinery, generators and other goods that need to be forwarded fast (by air) but don't fit into the holds of passenger aircraft. That will be another form of specialization in air freight, with a number of main-deck capacity providers concentrating increasingly on this segment, predominantly charter airlines operating large freighters.

New forms of transportation will also gain ground, for instance rail transport across the Eurasian land bridge. What began some years ago as an experiment has meanwhile become an attractive option to sea and also air freight even for carrying goods like printers, laptops and IT components, for example. The cargo trains operating between China and central/western Europe are running like clockwork – both ways. In the event that political disturbances between Russia and the West won't hamper these transports they will definitely gain ground since an increasing number of global logistics heavyweights (DHL, DB Schenker, Hellmann and others) but also medium-sized European and Chinese agents make increasing use of this mode of carriage. It can be expected that transport across the Eurasian land bridge will increasingly challenge the combined sea–air transports via Dubai and other ports in the Middle East due to time and cost advantages.

Generally speaking it can be expected that air freight will play a dominant role on intra-Asian routes, outgrowing other markets in the near future. Also Africa will get on the cargo map, with Latin America emerging strong. This will change traditional east–west trade lanes that played the first fiddle in air freight during the last 50 or so years, including trans-Pacific transport between East Asia and North America.

In Europe it can be expected that a single European sky, although much demanded by the aviation industry but blocked by the egoism of a number of EU members, will take another decade or even longer to be realized. It's doubtful that the perception of the broad public and particularly the politicians' views will change by realizing that this part of the (saturated) world is increasingly falling behind when it comes to building modern and sufficient ground infrastructure for aviation, say no to further night flight bans (unlike the Frankfurt disaster), and take necessary measures to secure the future of this vital industry, which in contrast to other business segments is constantly growing.

A bright future can be attested to road feeder services, predominantly within Europe. This is mainly because carriers tend to bundle their traffic on hubs like FRA, CDG, AMS or LHR. If so, exports produced in other regions have to be brought to the major European gateways. Road carriage is the only way, despite all talk about ecological-friendly rail transports, to get the goods from their origins to the next major hub that offers abundant traffic and connectivity.

Finally, it must be mentioned that air traffic unlike most other modes of transports is highly vulnerable to severe disruptions, be they security threats, political rifts, fast-rising fuel prices or other possible risks lurking around the corner. The eruption of the Icelandic volcano, Eyjafjallajokull, in March 2010, paralysing nearly the whole of Europe for almost a week, caused a total standstill of aviation. It should be a warning to all those that play with political or even military fire.

Fred Smith

Comments from Fred Smith, founder and CEO, Federal Express, from his speech at the 2014 IATA World Cargo Symposium in Los Angeles.

FedEx founder Fred Smith has warned that 'the golden age' of double-digit air cargo growth is unlikely to return due to trade protectionism, higher fuel costs and the rapid growth in belly-hold capacity: 'The big reason why international trade is not growing is the rise of protectionism, not just in China but in the rest of the world.'

In a keynote speech, Smith cited a 23 per cent increase in 'trade-inhibiting measures' by the leading nations since the economic crisis year of 2009, naming countries as diverse as Argentina, Russia and Canada in adopting 'beggar thy neighbour' restrictions on trade. He called on the airline industry to put pressure on politicians to end trade protectionism, which 'stifles competition and innovation while limiting consumer choice'. Other factors that have seen air cargo volumes falter include the miniaturization of electrical products, with less weight being transported.

> The key to global prosperity in the future must be to simplify regulations and restrictions that stifle and slow down international trade. Unfortunately the post-2008 recession has brought us into an era of protectionism with many countries passing new regulations designed to keep imports down whilst boosting their own exports. Free trade has become very elusive.
>
> For air cargo the advent of new mega-sized container ships which will be able to pass through the Panama Canal has created a new logistics culture where manufacturers can plan slow-steaming inventories which will deliver goods when needed at vastly lower cost. The B777, 767 and A330 are now allowing dramatically lower air freight costs which help to combat the threat.
>
> We must continue to work hard and efficiently, whilst pressuring politicians to open up our markets for more free trade. As the famous baseball player Yogi Berra stated, 'the future ain't what it used to be'.

Dieter Haltmayer

Dieter Haltmayer is President and CEO of Quick Cargo Services, a medium-sized independent freight forwarder based in Frankfurt with branches throughout Germany.

My view of the future of air cargo

I have been in the air cargo business for the last 50 years. There is no comparison between yesterday and today. When I started with BEA/BOAC, we still operated the Comet 4, DC 3 and Viscounts. Cargo was loaded by hand into the cargo holds. There were no pallets or containers; LD 3 or LD 7, they came later. Air waybills were typed on old typewriters and instead of e-mail we worked with teleprinters and tapes. The cargo manifest had to be typed and was duplicated on a special machine. The warehouse had no electronic systems. The air freight rates were high and forwarders received 5 per cent commission.

Today all this has changed. Today we work with electronic AWBs, now even paperless AWBs. The cargo manifest comes out of the computer printer. Pre-advices go by e-mail or direct from the computer to the consignee. Large cargo aircraft containers guarantee a fast ground time for the aircraft, but I also see a negative development in that freight rates are dealt on the free market with fuel surcharges which cannot be specified but the customer must accept. Security surcharges differ with every airline. Scanning of each piece is needed to make sure that no bombs are loaded. The computer age is costly and I see more growth with the ocean carriers rather than with the airlines. Freighter operations are a loss business for the air carriers, bearing in mind the increasing capacity available on the passenger aircraft.

Today the documentation and instructions kill the future of air freight. The general cargo becomes the domain of the global forwarding agents and the niche business will be part of the mid-size forwarding agents. IATA calculates 5 per cent increase worldwide, but the present political world situation hurts our industry very much. Around 50 per cent of the market coverage is controlled by companies like DHL Worldwide, FedEx, TNT and UPS; 25 per cent by logistics providers, eg Schenker, K&N, Panalpina; 20 per cent by 20–25 global operating forwarders like UTI SDV, EGL; and only 5 per cent market share remains for niche players and highly specialized services.

To be successful as a mid-size company like Quick Cargo Service we need a global strategy. Alliances and partnerships are the core strategy of our success today and in the future. We have to form alliances and have to recruit highly qualified service partners all over the globe. These alliances give us the ability to offer an excellent service worldwide. Each member of the alliance remains financially independent for joint developed business.

To compete with the top logistic providers we formed an alliance under the name of IGLU meaning, 'Association of common interests in air freight'. The objective is to pool freight at home at two hubs of Frankfurt and Munich in order to remain competitive in the market in the face of a growing concentration of preferred partners on the part of some carriers. IGLU vs individual companies, competitive vs larger consolidators, secure capacity access, better rate structure, higher loading priority with carriers, guaranteed departure and arrival time, better bargaining position through contract rates development of joint IT systems. The IT technology is fully competitive with the global players, track and tracing is working; e-freight and e-booking are a must and the requirements must be fulfilled if we want to succeed in the market.

Unfortunately the continuous new requirements to keep the supply chain 100 per cent on the cost saving side are very time-consuming and expensive. We wonder how a small or mid-size company is able to keep track and follow the requirements. We have to invest time and training for our staff to fulfil all the requirements, which are also very costly. To be honest the future for a mid-size company is not very bright. The political situation does not contribute to the expectations that the market situation will change in the near future.

Michael Sales

The future is a challenge

As world events are showing with increasing speed and volatility, realistic planning within the supply chain is becoming more challenging, despite the use of highly scientific business models and computer-based predictions. The shooting down of a civilian airliner by terrorists or unknown military antagonists, a major earthquake or an international outbreak of disease can have an alarming and immediate effect on social patterns and economies. While companies try to put in place contingency plans to cover such emergencies, we simply cannot anticipate such disasters. I believe that such events will continue to have a significant effect.

Thanks to the emergence of globalization of both supply and markets, efficient transport systems will become even more vital. When time is factored into a transport decision, the higher price of air transportation can bring better cost-efficiency in the overall end-to-end process. Inventory management and logistics are key components of any modern supply chain operation. Manufacturers and retailers are able to economize by decreasing the inventory held on their books. Components and parts are only produced on demand and on a just-in-time (JIT) delivery basis. Speed to customer is vital, as is getting the product to market and staying competitive. Management of the inventory-to-sales ratio is becoming a science in itself and is key to achieving optimal cost efficiency in inventory management. Today the supply chains of a product, rather than the product itself, are the competitive edge.

Fighting off the wolves

Apart from the problems inflicted on aviation by terrorists, natural disasters and economic cycles, climbing oil prices continue to be a challenge, not only by increasing the actual cost of transportation, but at the same time by diminishing consumer demand for all the normal day-to-day goods – a large element of the final price of household goods is transport costs. Oil prices are no longer demand-driven. Artificially controlled supply coupled with political pressure and tensions is keeping the oil price high and unpredictable. Today's aircraft are vastly more cost-efficient and productive than previously but will continue to depend largely on fossil fuels, despite experimentation with other fuel sources.

Air cargo has to make itself much more cost-effective to justify its high cost. The march of mobile phone communication and the internet has made information instantly available in real time. The daily use of these systems for operating the supply chain should eliminate error and waste in the future. The worsening situation in the Middle East and the clash of conflicting religions and cultures will have a major impact on world trade and will require some very strong negotiating between the conflicting groups to find some reasonable solution.

New generation

To combat these negative factors, the air freight industry is taking steps to address the situation. A combined team approach amongst the various bodies and authorities is beginning to bear fruit. As cargo is more than ever tied to passenger routes and aircraft, it has become a vital part of airlines' revenue and profitability. Overall, our world, our industry is going through a renewal process. The new generation of managers entering logistics and freight for-warding will find new solutions for this truly global enterprise. Even small companies that transport primarily within a particular country will have to develop international business relations with correspondent companies in other countries, probably through trade groups such as WCA. Bigger companies will have networks across the world. For anyone looking to build a career with a challenge, overseas job opportunities are often an attractive prospect, providing a glimpse of opportunity and possibility that can be as aspirational as it is exciting. The air freight business can offer these opportunities.

Tony Tyler, IATA's chief executive, comments: 'Logistics has become an even more intensely competitive sector. Shippers value faster end-to-end transit times, greater reliability and improved efficiency.'

Stan Wraight

TIACA Leadership Training – all about change

For the past five years I have been very passionate about the need to 'give something back' to this industry, one that has been so good to me. Being such a cyclical business, air cargo has seen a real brain drain either through design, or through no fault of its own as one crisis after another hit the margins of airlines, forcing cutback after cutback.

Many have tried to effect change, and they still are trying, but I saw something in TIACA that existed nowhere else and that was the diversity of its membership in the logistics supply chain around air cargo, and the very real passion of its executives who all donate their time trying to make the industry more viable, more profitable and therefore more sustainable. It took a long time, but finally the first TIACA Leadership course designed for young up and coming managers in the supply chain took place in Amsterdam.

They were fantastic, just as we had hoped, and the participants went away with glowing testimonials as to why. For the first time ever in one room we put together a bank, forwarder, ground handling companies, a scheduled passenger airline and an all-cargo airline, and for three full days we talked, debated and informed.

For sure the top-down issues were covered such as an overview of supply chains, including a customer guest speaker, marketing principles, understanding financial statements, business conduct and ethics, amongst other topics. However, what really differentiated this course was the dialogue between the different interests in the room on how we could eliminate days from the supply chain for air cargo; what new product/market combinations could look like that would facilitate both revenue improvement for all parties and also improve load factors for airlines; how to get costs out of the supply chain; and lastly, how those young managers in the room could go back to their companies and help start that process and grow in their jobs at the same time. What was a personal highlight was being in a room full of young managers, and watch them absorb all those ideas and experiences from the trainers and 'veterans' who donated their time.

If air cargo is to return to being a core business for scheduled passenger airlines and profitable for all cargo airlines, we need more innovative thinking and more passing on of the lessons of history and what is possible going forward to the next generation. They have to learn and then get out there and make it happen. And I believe TIACA has created a perfect platform to do this due to its diverse industrial membership.

Product innovation is missing in our business today, and global load factors prove that. We hear a lot about special products for pharma, and other higher-yielding commodities. But why is no one talking about a seven-day product, a 15-day product, and that does not have to be sea–air! I want the next modal shift discussions to take place in sea freight conferences, not air cargo ones, and it can be done!

Worldwide we see an average air cargo load factor of just over 50 per cent; that is such a tremendous waste of asset value. Why we don't have innovation and progress is relatively easy to see: too many separate silos in the supply chain that don't do anything but try and maximize their margins just to survive, and too many airlines that have just given up and are no longer investing in cargo or management who are willing to innovate.

'Blame the recession' is the standard cry, yet passenger traffic is growing at double digits in the same period. What does the cargo sector of this industry do – change like the passenger divisions did with innovation and new products? No, what we did was same old, same old, and wait hopefully for someone else to fix the problems.

E-commerce is the fastest-growing business in transportation, and the post offices are putting products on the shelf to facilitate their clients' needs and grab the lion's share of this huge market potential. When was the last time you heard an airline announce a product that caters to e-commerce, and its need for low weight breaks, low minimums, handling solutions at airports? The answer is never!

Low-cost airlines did not grow to the powerhouses they are today by stealing clients from the legacy carriers; they grew by creating new products, new models that put people in seats who had never flown before, to places they had never been. They made their products very easy to use, and tackled all the issues that stood in their way. Where is that entrepreneurial spirit gone in air cargo?

The boardrooms of major airlines are always dominated by people who have one duty only: to do what is best for the carrier. Unless the new generation of air cargo leaders take the challenge and change, introduce innovative and dynamic business models into their companies' boardrooms and create product/market combinations that fill those empty bellies, the circle of decline will continue.

It's not just the airlines that will suffer; everyone in the supply chain that depends on air cargo will suffer as well. That's why the TIACA training is so important: everyone in that room understood how working together to tackle the industry's inefficiencies could lead to better business for the whole chain.

It's our responsibility now to take it to the next step, and we will do it. This organization deserves all the support the industry can give it, and I urge more people to join.

Ram Menen

Former Head of Emirates SkyCargo and one-time president of TIACA, now retired

The 21st century is a whole new era and a whole new world. It is critical that all aspects of the industry embrace the future and let the future drive today. It is very critical that all are better aware and equipped to deal with the changes and challenges. The better aware one is, the better equipped one is to not only manage the changes, but also to drive the evolution of our business. Different commodities require different transportation requirements. Gone are the days of one size fits all. Changes in requirements are happening in real time these days. 3D printing is going to bring in a whole plethora of changes to the manufacturing and consumption process. This will trigger changes in many other areas that could create some challenges, but also more new opportunities. We tend to operate in uncharted territory more often than ever. Markets are more volatile and economic cycles tend to linger longer with higher frequency. Those who are able to anticipate change and support the change effectively will be the winners.

The law – organizations and regulations governing international aviation

15

The global aviation industry can only function if it adheres to a system of regulations and controls supported by a network of internationally agreed rules. These rules govern all civil aviation operations including ground activities, flight operations, safety, border controls, liabilities and environmental restrictions. The ultimate aim of these controls is to ensure the safe operation of this vast and complex industrial sector.

From the earliest days it was evident that without worldwide agreements, it would not be possible to operate even domestically but more important internationally. The Paris International Air Convention, introduced in 1922, defined the sovereign control of national airspace. The concept of the right to fly over an individual country's airspace was admitted. This treaty, containing nine sections, dealt with the nationality of aircraft, certificates of airworthiness, patents and permissions for take-off and landing. The International Commission of Air Navigation (ICAN) based in Paris, provided a base of legal, technical and meteorological services.

A conference held in Paris in October 1925 was attended by representatives from 43 countries. Preliminary work was carried out in preparation for a second conference to be held in Warsaw in 1929. The resulting Warsaw Convention became the most important agreement in the aviation industry.

The Warsaw Convention

The Convention was signed in 1929 by 152 different parties and came into force in 1933. It aimed to regulate liability for international carriage of people, their luggage or goods carried by aircraft for financial reward. It also defined international carriage, necessary documentation, the liability limitations of the carrier as well as jurisdiction. In 1955, a review by the International Civil Aviation Organization (ICAO) resulted in the Hague Protocol being adopted by the ICAO council. In 1955, the two conventions were turned into one, known simply as the Warsaw Convention.

Liabilities

The Convention provided protection and compensation to passengers and freight operators but it was at the same time agreed that part of the risk should be down to the users of air transport. Although such a complex regulatory framework was inevitably open to considerable debate, the Convention remained the basis for settling litigation until recent times. Several important countries, including Germany, the Soviet Union, China and the United States did not join but instead formed the Pan-American Convention on Commercial Aviation, which was signed by 22 countries in Havana in 1928. The Chicago Convention couldn't resolve the issue of who flies where, however, and this has resulted in the thousands of bilaterals in existence today. The benchmark standard for the early bilaterals was the 1946 United States–United Kingdom Bermuda Agreement. The levels of compensation for passenger injuries have risen over the years but are still a matter of international dispute.

The Montreal Convention 1999 (MC99) was offered as an alternative solution to unify the varied liability obligations that arose since the original 1929 Convention. For cargo, both origin and destination countries must have ratified MC99. If this is not the case, a shipment operates under the lowest common denominator.

The IATA e-AWB multilateral agreement has added pressure for the adoption of MC99. The agreement allows airlines and freight forwarders to sign once with IATA and in effect enter into e-AWB agreements with all other parties to the agreement. By speeding up e-freight implementation it will force states to consider adopting MC99 sooner rather than later.

Regulatory bodies

The air cargo industry is responsible for the safe and reliable transport of US\$6.5 trillion worth of goods annually, goods that are traded by every industry imaginable and that come in all shapes and sizes. This requires the fulfilment of a wide range of conditions of transport, from constant, specific temperature ranges to enhanced speed or security. The industry is truly global and highly fragmented, complex and challenged by economic, technological, environmental and regulatory factors.

The International Air Cargo Association (TIACA) is the only global association open to all stakeholders in the industry and counts shippers, forwarders, airlines, integrators, handlers, IT providers, truckers and educational institutes amongst its members. TIACA is a not-for-profit organization which reinvests 100 per cent of its income in promoting and supporting its members and the vital role they play in world commerce. Its activities fall under three major headings: advocacy and industry affairs, networking and the organization of events, and education and knowledge sharing. TIACA therefore fulfils a unique and vital role as the voice of the industry, engaging with regulators and responding to the demands of shippers. While various segments of the industry are well represented by their own associations, TIACA requires a collaborative approach in order to facilitate a sustainable and connected global industry. TIACA is the global organization for all users and participants in the air cargo industry (see **www.tiaca.org**).

IATA: International Air Transport Association

The most important organization controlling aviation is IATA, headquartered in Montreal, Canada and Geneva, Switzerland. Originally IATA consisted of 57 airlines from 31 countries. Much of IATA's early work was technical and it provided input to the newly created International Civil Aviation Organization (ICAO), which was reflected in the annexes of the Chicago Convention, the international treaty that still governs the conduct of international air transport. IATA was also charged by the governments with setting a coherent fare structure that was intended to eliminate cut-throat competition but also looked after the interests of the passengers. The first Traffic Conference was held in 1947 in Rio de Janeiro and was able to reach unanimous agreement on 400 resolutions over the following 60 years. It has evolved from a trade association into a multifunctional organization. IATA has established itself as the voice of the aviation industry, launching a number of important programmes and lobbying governments in the interests of its members.

Safety is the number-one priority for IATA and the main initiative for achieving its goals is the IATA Operational Safety Audit (IOSA) and its successor, Enhanced IOSA. IOSA has also been mandated at state level by several countries. In 2012, aviation posted its safest year ever.

To promote collaboration between players involved in cargo logistics, including governments and Customs, the World Cargo Symposium (WCS), which is hosted by IATA, has become a major event at which decisions affecting the industry are taken. The Cargo division of IATA manages a wide range of activities and regulations that are vital for industry-wide operations, including dangerous goods, animal transportation, perishables and pharmaceuticals, security, Customs compliance and electronic documentation. Ongoing projects include, in collaboration with FIATA, the Cargo Agency Programme, which will address issues such as accreditation, training and supplier and buyer relations. The e-Cargo initiative attempts to introduce digital processing to increase speed and the replacement of paper documents.

To support regulators and strengthen supply chain security, IATA and the industry are working on various cargo security initiatives: the IATA Center of Excellence for Independent Validators, the Standard Consignment Security Declaration and Secure Freight. Acknowledging the need for the air cargo industry to develop long-term strategies and investments, IATA is working on several cargo sustainability initiatives tackling environmental, social and economic issues (details can be found on the IATA website: **www.iata.org**.)

ICAO: The International Civil Aviation Organization

ICAO develops policies and standards, undertakes compliance audits, performs studies and analyses, provides assistance and builds aviation capacity through many other activities and the cooperation of its member states and stakeholders. To achieve the sustainable growth of the global civil aviation system ICAO works with the Convention's 191 Signatory States and global industry and aviation organizations to develop international Standards and Recommended Practices (SARPs) which are then used by nations when they develop their legally binding national civil aviation regulations. There are currently over 10,000 SARPs reflected in the 19 Annexes to the Chicago Convention that ICAO oversees, and it is through these SARPs and ICAO's complementary policy, auditing and capacity-building efforts that today's global air transport network is able to operate over 100,000 daily flights safely, efficiently and securely in every region of the world. (See **www.icao.org** for more information.)

WCO: The World Customs Organization

WCO, established in 1952 as the Customs Cooperation Council (CCC), is an independent intergovernmental body whose mission is to enhance the effectiveness and efficiency of Customs administrations. Today, the WCO represents 179 Customs administrations across the globe that collectively process approximately 98 per cent of world trade. As the global centre of Customs expertise, the WCO is the only international organization with competence in Customs matters and can rightly call itself the voice of the international Customs community.

The WCO's governing body – the Council – relies on the competence and skills of a Secretariat and a range of technical and advisory committees to accomplish its mission. The Secretariat comprises over 100 international officials, technical experts and support staff of various nationalities.

As a forum for dialogue and exchange of experiences between national Customs delegates, the WCO offers its members a range of conventions and other international instruments, as well as technical assistance and training services provided either directly by the Secretariat, or with its participation. The Secretariat also actively supports its members in their endeavours to modernize and build capacity within their national Customs administrations.

Besides the vital role played by the WCO in stimulating the growth of legitimate international trade, its efforts to combat fraudulent activities are also recognized internationally. The partnership approach championed by the WCO is one of the keys to building bridges between Customs administrations and their partners. By promoting the emergence of an honest, transparent and predictable Customs environment, the WCO directly contributes to the economic and social wellbeing of its members.

Finally, in an international environment characterized by instability and the ever-present threat of terrorist activity, the WCO's mission to enhance the protection of society and national territory, and to secure and facilitate international trade, takes on its full meaning. (For more information see **www.wcoomd.org**.)

FIATA: *Fédération Internationale des Associations de Transitaires et Assimilés*

FIATA, a non-governmental organization, was founded in Vienna, Austria on 31 May 1926. Today it represents an industry covering approximately 40,000 forwarding and logistics firms, also known as the 'Architects of transport', employing around 8–10 million people in 150 countries.

FIATA has consultative status with the Economic and Social Council (ECOSOC) of the United Nations (inter alia ECE, ESCAP, ESCWA), the United Nations Conference on Trade and Development (UNCTAD), and the UN Commission on International Trade Law (UNCITRAL). It is recognized as representing the freight forwarding industry by many other governmental organizations and authorities, private international organizations in the field of transport such as the International Chamber of Commerce (ICC), the International Air Transport Association (IATA), the International Union of Railways (UIC), the International Road Transport Union (IRU), the World Customs Organization (WCO) and the World Trade Organization (WTO). (For more information see **www.fiata.com**.)

CCA: The Cool Chain Association

The CCA is a non-profit organization, founded in 2003, with the aim of reducing wastage and improving the quality, efficiency and value of the temperature-sensitive supply chain by facilitating and enabling vertical and horizontal collaboration, education and innovation amongst our members and stakeholders.

ACI: Airports Council International

The ACI is the only global trade representative of the world's airports. Established in 1991, ACI represents airports' interests with governments and international organizations, develops standards, policies and recommended practices for airports, and provides information and training opportunities to raise standards around the world. It aims to provide the public with a safe, secure, efficient and environmentally responsible air transport system.

It is governed by the ACI Governing Board. ACI World is located in Montreal, Canada. ACI works on a daily basis with the International Civil Aviation Organization and is a member of the Air Transport Action Group.

In 2012, ACI member airports worldwide handled 92.5 million metric tonnes of cargo and 79 million movements. ACI reported 573 members operating 1,751 airports in 174 countries and territories, representing over 95 per cent of global airport traffic. ACI members are owners or operators, other than airlines, of one or more civil airports with commercial air services. (For more information see **www.aci.aero**.)

TAPA: Transported Asset Protection Association

TAPA is a unique forum that unites global manufacturers, logistics providers, freight carriers, law enforcement agencies, and other stakeholders with the common aim of reducing losses from international supply chains. (For more information see **www.tapaemea.com**.)

National bodies

Each country has its own regulatory organizations. *The World Civil Aviation Authorities Directory* provides a comprehensive list by country (see **www.airlineupdate.com**).

GLOSSARY OF COMMON AIR FREIGHT TERMS

ACMI   Aircraft, crew, maintenance, insurance (wet lease).

air cargo   Goods carried in an aircraft.

air freight   The loading of cargo into an aircraft; often synonymous with air cargo.

airside   Those parts of an airport controlled by the Customs authorities that are inaccessible to unauthorized personnel.

all-cargo carrier   An airline that does not carry passengers.

apron   Aircraft parking area, for refuelling and the handling of cargo, baggage and mail.

AWB   Air waybill, giving full details of the cargo.

block space   Air freight forwarders pre-book space with airlines.

break-bulk   Outsize or overweight cargo that will not fit in standard containers or pallets.

CASS   The airlines' account settlement system.

Civil Reserve Air Fleet (CRAF)   US military use of civilian service providers of freighters.

code share   An agreement whereby an airline sells capacity on another carrier's service. Generally applicable only to passenger services.

combination carrier   An airline that operates both passenger and cargo services.

consignee   The person or organization to whom cargo is being sent.

consolidation   When the cargo from two or more shippers is carried in a single shipment.

CTK   Cargo-Tonne-Kilometre; a key airline performance indicator.

curfew   Those hours, usually at night, when flights to and from an airport are banned or restricted.

dangerous goods   Cargo that can only be carried under strictly regulated circumstances and on specific flights.

door to door   The movement of cargo from consignor to consignee by a single operator (usually an express operator or integrator).

dry lease   Lease of an aircraft, with the lessee operator providing its own crew, maintenance and insurance.

e-AWB   Electronic air waybill.

EDI   Electronic Data Interchange.

FAA   Federal Aviation Administration (United States).

FF   Freight forwarder.

flag carrier   The national airline of a country (often government-owned).

GHA   Ground Handling Agent. (Another term in use is General Handling Agent.)
GSSA   General Sales and Service Agent.

HAWB   House air waybill.
hub and spoke   The route network where smaller aircraft feed cargo into a main hub which in turn is linked to other main hubs around the world by big long-haul aircraft.

IATA   International Air Transport Association.
ICAO   International Civil Aviation Organization.
integrator   An air express operator, usually with its own hub and spoke.

JIT   Just-in-time.

KPI   Key Performance Indicator.

MAWB   Master air waybill.
MTOW   Maximum take-off weight.
multimodal   The use of more than one transport mode, such as air, sea, road or rail.

noise footprint   The sound map made by an aircraft, usually when landing at or take-off from an airport in built-up areas.

off-line   A destination not served by a scheduled airline.
oversize cargo   Cargo that will not fit in a standard container or in a specific aircraft.

pallet   A ULD on which cargo is placed prior to being loaded into an aircraft.

reefer   Refrigerated vehicle or container.
RFS   Road feeder service.

split charter   Where two or more consignors share space on a chartered aircraft.

tech stop   Where an aircraft lands at an airport prior to arriving at its destination airport, usually for refuelling purposes.
TIACA   The International Air Cargo Association.
tonne   Metric weight: 1,000 kg.
traffic rights   Intergovernmental agreements stating which airlines may fly on specific routes between countries.

ULD   Unit Load Device (aircraft container).

WCO   World Customs Organization.
wet lease   See ACMI and dry lease.

INDEX

Note: page numbers in *italics* indicate figures, photos/pictures or tables.